Earth Warriors
O R A C L E

Rise of the Soul Tribe
of Sacred Guardians & Inspired Visionaries

ALANA FAIRCHILD

BLUE ANGEL®
PUBLISHING

This printing 2020
Copyright © 2018 Alana Fairchild
Artwork Copyright © 2018 Isabel Bryna

Published by Blue Angel Publishing®
80 Glen Tower Drive, Glen Waverley,
Victoria, Australia 3150
E-mail: info@blueangelonline.com
Website: www.blueangelonline.com

Edited by Jamie Morris

Blue Angel is a registered trademark of Blue Angel Gallery, Pty. Ltd.

ISBN: 978-1-925538-29-8

There is a river flowing now very fast. It is so great and swift that there are those who will be afraid. They will try to hold on to the shore. They will feel they are torn apart and will suffer greatly.

Know the river has its destination. The elders say we must let go of the shore, push off into the middle of the river, keep our eyes open, and our heads above water. And I say, see who is in there with you and celebrate. At this time in history, we are to take nothing personally, least of all ourselves. For the moment that we do, our spiritual growth and journey comes to a halt.

The time for the lone wolf is over. Gather yourselves! Banish the word 'struggle' from your attitude and your vocabulary. All that we do now must be done in a sacred manner and in celebration.

We are the ones we've been waiting for.

– Attributed to an unnamed Hopi elder,
Hopi Nation, Oraibi, Arizona

EARTH WARRIORS are the healers and transformational leaders for a more beautiful world. They destabilise the status quo with their innovative attitude and higher consciousness, defying convention and living from the heart. They are not afraid of change – they embrace it and lead the human race forward in to new ways of thinking, being and living in this world for the greatest good.

Earth Warriors seek love as their leader and wisdom as their guide. They question authority and respect only what is shown to be wise and true. They nourish conscious community relationships and envision a hopeful future for all upon the earth, connecting with their soul tribe to bring that vision to life.

Earth Warriors know what is true in their own hearts, and they refuse to be conditioned by mass consciousness into fear, apathy, complacency or overwhelm and despair. They have enormous positive energy within and a passionate desire for meaningful contribution and constructive sacred purpose in this world.

Earth Warriors love our planet with passionate devotion and fierce wisdom. Willing to cause a stir for the right cause, the Earth Warriors bring truth out of darkness, when others who trade in fear would wish to keep it hidden. Earth Warriors are the wise guides showing the way towards our world of the future that is bright and honouring of life.

These are the new world leaders-in-the-making, the solution-creators. They are stirring up beautiful trouble to challenge mainstream views with higher consciousness and healing change, and they hold an important role in love's revolution on our planet. These are the safe hands holding the earth as she goes through a massive paradigm shift into new consciousness. The *Earth Warriors Oracle* helps you tap in to your creativity, courage and optimism so you can fulfil your sacred purpose, making a real and positive difference in your own life and for the greatest good in our world.

We are these Earth Warriors, this soul tribe of sacred community that honours life, connection and relationship, refuses to bow down to authority and, instead, dares to define – and live by – what matters most. We recognise that our courage and truth-speaking, our way of living and being, create a light by which humanity can find its way into authentic, compassionate and wise relationship with ourselves and all of life.

The power and ways are given to us to be passed on to others.
– Fools Crow, Ceremonial Chief, Teton Sioux

This deck has been created to connect you with a loving combination of divine feminine wisdom, whilst awakening divine masculine strength within you. Whether you are a man or a woman, you have feminine and masculine sides to your soul. When you learn how to honour and utilise both aspects, your empowerment and creative presence increases and your ability to fulfil your sacred life purpose, to know what that is and to just boldly get on with living it, awakens, too.

You can use this deck for your own personal guidance. It can help you gain courage and inspiration for your life journey. It is especially helpful for guidance on your life mission and divine purpose. It will support you in creating the sort of energy that is magnetic to the people, opportunities and information that can assist you in taking the next steps on your life path – even if you have absolutely no idea what that could look like right now. The Divine knows who you are and what you are here to accomplish and will guide you every step of the way into joyful fulfilment for the greatest good of all life upon this earth.

We are all indigenous to this earth. Humanity needs the strength, wisdom and love of those who know how to be uplifted, encouraged, mobilised and connected, how to be supported by spiritual light and truth, how to fight like wild divine lions for what truly matters, the only things that truly matter – and *win*. Our light and wisdom must prevail. Our time has come.

Contents

Introduction

GUARDIANS OF THE NEW WORLD

A new world is being born. It is founded upon community and wisdom, instead of exploitation and short-sightedness; upon love and higher consciousness, instead of fear, hate and greed. This new world is gaining ground, becoming stronger, yet it also needs its protectors during this precious and important time of birth. These protectors are those of us who will ensure that this new world continues to grow, remains true to divine wisdom and is available for all who wish to leave the old ways behind them. Earth Warriors are the protectors, the guardians, guides and way-showers for the new world – and they are here to show its people how to prosper and thrive in harmony with the wisdom of life.

WHO ARE EARTH WARRIORS?

In love with nature and open to innovative, out-of-the-ordinary ways of thinking, Earth Warriors know there are issues in ourselves, our lives and our world that need to change. Instead of being overcome by despair or defeat, the Earth Warrior rises up as a believer, a rebel, a fighter and an optimist. With trust in the power of healing and divine spirit, they embrace their own healing process, knowing that as they do so they will be increasingly empowered as a catalyst for healing change in the world, too.

Earth Warriors are evolved souls bringing the Divine Masculine and Divine Feminine together in a paradigm shift of consciousness and action that will secure a positive future for all life on Earth. These old souls have a spiritual lineage reaching back through numerous spiritual civilisations on Earth and beyond. That soul history has given them wisdom and the understanding of how we can create a successful civilisation that will thrive and endure, with love. They know that we need creative solutions to human problems, and that reality based in higher-awareness requires innovative development in all fields, including science and technology, so as to benefit and support life. Through the teachings of the civilisation of Atlantis, Earth Warriors have developed a love of innovative systems and technology. Through the Lemurian civilisation, they have learned that the honouring of feminine wisdom ensures that technology will be helpful in the short and long term, becoming a positive legacy of human intelligence – rather than a testament to selfishness and greed that becomes anti-life and leads to destruction.

Earth Warriors know that a healed relationship between science and spirituality, health and education and all other disciplines and facets of human existence, working together for the greatest good, is going to help humanity far more than a wounded, fear-based competition for supposed superiority. Earth Warriors know that humanity needs the light of knowledge – education and unbiased useful information – to be combined with divine love, so that knowledge can be used for inspired, helpful, empowered and loving action in the world. Earth Warriors have the unusual ability to embrace a multi-disciplinary approach. They are able to integrate ideas from many traditions, fields of enquiry and sources of knowledge and collaborate to find the wisdom-solutions that we can only discover through working together and for the common cause of life itself.

Where those in fear may deny difficult truths, the Earth Warriors say, 'Okay, this is happening. What are we going to do about it? How can we combine our abilities, knowledge and skills to do something creative and amazing with this opportunity for healing?' They are spiritual, they are practical, they are solution-creators, and they willingly invite divine love to assist them every step of the way.

Combining the wisdom of the Divine Feminine and the strength of the Divine Masculine to sanctify and defend what matters most, Earth Warriors are the pioneers of the new world. They are our hope for the future. They are you and me.

POLITICS HAS BECOME A QUESTION OF CONSCIOUSNESS

The new politics has become a question not of left nor right but of consciousness. This is an exciting time filled with possibility. Whilst those in fear focus on the unavoidable chaos of the creative birth of a new world order, those in divine love see opportunities to do something different, to play with optimism and creativity.

Developing everything from new forms of housing, production, recycling and up-cycling, to cradle-to-cradle production and strategic systems change, there are many who have long since diagnosed the problems humanity has created and are already responding actively with empowered, fresh optimism to support life and be sustainable. These new approaches, in some cases, actually shift human culture from just surviving and minimising harm to the earth to thriving and actively enhancing and improving the environment through how we live. For those that want to live with integrity and peace, rather than guilt, anger and shame, this is a time of light piercing through the darkness.

Whilst others are still in denial that there even is a problem, arguing about whether or not global warming is even a thing, others have pioneered a way forward. These bright, capable, smart and savvy people are shifting towards an optimistic, adventurous, willing-to-mix-it-up consciousness. This enables them to innovate into harmonious, practical alternatives and support the continuation of this positive movement for genuine change on the planet. The shift starts with attitude. If we are locked in depression or, even further down the chain of awareness, denial, then nothing can happen there.

Fortunately, critical mass theory teaches us that we don't all need to get it in order to shift what isn't working. The more the merrier, yes, but those of us who can see and are willing to go through the discomfort of confronting what isn't working in our lives – and have the courage to be creative and embrace change – can keep the positive momentum going. So, we can legitimately cultivate hope in our hearts and minds, and from that place of authentic optimism, make changes, big and small, in our way of being in this world. We can also encourage each other to become the birth mothers and fathers of a far more loving and wise new world order.

THE DIVINE FEMININE SPEAKS

The fundamental truth that Earth Warriors understand is that nature is generous. To exploit her is not necessary for survival. She gives so much, and when we learn to operate in loving relationship with her as a living, wise mother, our needs are met, and we don't destroy the planet with ignorance or greed.

Many years ago, I had a dream of an ocean tide pulling back to reveal a precious and perfect lyrebird feather at the base of the ocean before my feet. That feather was so ready for the taking, I reached down to pick it up, believing it was meant for me. Suddenly, a lyrebird appeared out of nowhere (as tends to happen in dreams) and gently, but also firmly, held my forefinger in its beak. I understood it was saying 'no' to me picking up this feather.

That dream brought numerous teachings into my awareness in the years following. The Sacred Feminine often teaches us through dreams, which is a way through which she can reveal her mysteries and truths without our conscious mind obstructing her with logic, pride, vanity or fear. One of the teachings that dream brought to me was a profound understanding of the difference between receiving and taking, even if what we are taking is something we could rightfully claim if we exerted some effort and the act of taking doesn't appear to be harming anyone or anything in the process.

In our modern culture, the word 'no' is sometimes considered inferior to the concept of 'yes'. Don't get me wrong – I am a massive fan of the unimpeded, passionate 'YES!' to the Universe. However, I understand that, in that absolute invitation, we will be given what we need. From time to time, that will include a wisdom that asks for restraint or pause. I believe that each one of us learning how to honour this in our own personal lives is a powerful antidote to the dangerous entitlement culture operating in modern humanity. The hallmark of that culture is a belief that if you *can* do something, then you *should* do it – and merely wanting something is enough to consider you are owed it (and therefore entitled to take it for yourself). That sort of attitude places power over love and wisdom, and we know what a devastating outcome such a perverse priority causes in ourselves and the world: disease, destruction, famine, pain and suffering in endless ways.

It is my understanding that the placement of power over love is what separates the human soul from the real, loving, generous and even (when necessary) restraining, life-honouring wisdom of the Divine Feminine – both in nature and in our own souls, through dreams and intuitive inner knowing. That placement of power over love causes disruption in our own soul and, from that, in the world. When we correct the pain in the soul with wisdom, the healed soul becomes the medicine to correct the state of the world.

Many modern souls are trying to claw their way back into correct relationship with the earth and her sacred feminine wisdom through tribal wisdom – whether that be perhaps somewhat unconsciously expressed in a desire for tribal-inspired fashion or in a deep need for an experience of the ways of those indigenous peoples that are willing to share their culture with those outside of it.

Passion for Eastern mysticism can also express this need, particularly when that passion seeks out aspects of spiritual traditions that profoundly revere the Divine Feminine. These may include the Hindu path of Divine Mother worship or the Taoist path of surrendered, joyful harmony in the ways of nature and life itself. Being drawn to shamanism, drumming, conscious or ecstatic dance, even yoga can lead the soul to find a pathway back into truth. There the soul feeds itself with genuine nourishment, as it comes out of the head and the terrors of belief systems that venerate power and puts roots back down into the earth.

Earth Warriors are those that understand all human beings are indigenous to this earth, and yet the tribal peoples, each so beautifully unique and special in their differences, are precious and worthy of being safeguarded – even from our own curiosity-based tourism, when needs be! There is an understanding here that a wise 'no' from time to time helps a much bigger 'yes' unfold according to a wisdom greater than our own. We don't need to understand how it can all come together. Our sacred task is to tune in and learn to be guided by a greater wisdom than our own personal, immediate understanding of things. This is the essence of the universal tribal consciousness that wise souls yearn to sink into and live by.

There is so much beauty of creation in this world, so much that is worth protecting and honouring. The ability of love to heal and produce profound transformation is beyond compare. Such genuine and sustained transformation cannot be evoked by power or force, for those things will always evoke resistance, will always be subject to recurring battles for dominance that erupt during moments of weakness in the prevailing order. Yet love is not always quiet. She rallies and she is fierce – and she has anger and courage, too. What she also brings is joy. We must remember this so as to nourish ourselves always on this journey of alchemical activism for soul healing – in ourselves and the world. We can get rumpled and ruffled as we get amongst it, and yet we can also retain a joyful peace within the depths of our innermost being, a quiet, unassailable certainty that the way of wisdom shall ultimately prevail.

CLAIMING YOUR INDIGENOUS ROOTS TO THE EARTH MOTHER

Sometimes the problems of the world – and humanity's collective behaviour towards each other and the environment – can be so profoundly disturbing that the reaction is to switch off from it, to do our best to live our lives and make a difference without really feeling powerful enough, or informed enough, to know how to even begin to tackle the larger situation at hand. Some people react by denying it is happening at all, which is understandable but, ultimately, unnecessary and unhelpful.

We are at an end point, and of course those of us on the spiritual path know that end points signal birth. It is not a time to give up to hopelessness or despair. We can rally our wildness, our courage and our ferocious compassion to believe in love and to act as the fearless Earth Warrior, love's revolutionary. We can seek to use every one of our talents and spiritual abilities in service to what matters – life. Our wise use of the gifts we have been so generously given is part of our strength. We have the ability to live and be in a way that educates, empowers and rallies into conscious, constructive community those that are willing to take the divine journey.

Let the truth of your spirit fill your mind and heart. There is no need to shy away, to feel not informed enough or not up to the task. The purpose of this deck, at a practical level, is to help you feel the level of consciousness necessary to naturally attract the next piece of information, the people, situations, opportunities, education and experiences that you need to take your next steps. The Divine is a very helpful and willing, practical and miraculous teacher. All we need to do is be willing to participate. Everything else will be offered as we need it. I have seen and experienced this in my own life in countless ways – in unimaginable and amazing ways – again and again.

There are many Earth Warriors who have long been putting new systems into place, and there is much to be hopeful about. There are plenty of ways that each one of us can educate ourselves and others with joy, as we make the pleasurable, energising discovery that, with divine grace, human ingenuity and courage, we can not only recover from our mistakes and ignorance, but actually learn how to thrive in harmony with this planet. In doing so, we can generate a positive human legacy rather than a disturbing, destructive footprint.

The deck holds the promise that the Divine will provide all that is needed to the willing heart to fulfil your destiny as a wise warrior for love on this planet. Shed your old skins, leave behind hesitation and trust your heart and your divine connection as you now join us, becoming the Earth Warrior you were always destined to be. The battle cry of Earth's wise children unites us all. It evokes a passionate response from Spirit that brings sacred healing grace to our cause.

If we cannot own – and then move through – our shame and anger at how human beings have treated each other, especially our First Peoples, we cut ourselves off from vital, joyful energy that is necessary for a new way to evolve on this planet. To dig deep and learn to plug into the human collective with a sense of belonging, self-worth and capacity requires us to believe in the goodness that is within our souls. Creation, innovation and the energy to change our world starts with self-respect and forgiveness. The ability to work together to bring about healing change and restoration of sense, wisdom and balance through human activity on this planet is essential. If we are isolating ourselves out of an unresolved sense of shame, guilt or rage, then we are going to need to overcome that first. Then we can gain fuller access to our potential, redirecting that negative energy into positive outcomes.

If we so choose, each one of us can remember that we are all Earth's indigenous people, each one of us, with wild wisdom in our hearts. For some of us, the journey to remember that truth seems more arduous. But through taking that journey, we also gain a deep understanding of how to return to the feminine, which can be inspirational for others. It is something akin to the prodigal son returning home. As we claim our rightful place as one of the Earth Mother's divine children, we can allow ourselves to feel a sense of privilege that is not dysfunctional entitlement, but that is about belonging. When we allow ourselves to feel loved and to love without shame, guilt or fear, our ability to fight from the heart for our beloved increases in an extraordinary way. The walls come down, the bullshit gets called for what it is, and we clean up what needs cleaning up – together. Many hands make light work, as the expression goes. And, yes, let's read that on more than one level of uplifting and positive interpretation.

Together we have more energy. We have a sense of self confidence and worth that makes us more willing to try new things, to put our energy into causes and consciousness that mean something to our souls. We aren't hiding away in shame, afraid of the terrible past and caught up in feelings of inferiority and helplessness. Instead, we step forward, heart and mind wide open, saying, 'This is a damn mess, but I am going to see it as the chaos of creative rebirth – and with radical optimism and divine defiance I am going to do something constructive with this state of consciousness every day.' With the love and power of the Earth

Mother behind us, within us, we have the courage to honour that statement, to take the journey to grow and become a part of the solution, part of a beautiful future.

As enough of us remember and restore our sacred soul connection to the earth and open with empowering trust to our divine connection to Spirit, our human potential can be fulfilled. From that truly magnificent place, brilliant solutions can continue to grow and gain traction in our world.

Together, we can keep learning and growing, leaning on each other and the Divine, as we join the light of the new world, leaving the old ways behind us. It *is* happening now. This deck is your support to continue – or perhaps discover – your important role in this revolution of consciousness and loving, of inspired action upon our planet. It will help you remain at the right frequency as you become part of the shift in the world.

HOW TO USE THIS DECK

You can use this deck for your own personal guidance or for guiding others to gain courage and inspiration for one's life journey. It is especially helpful for guidance on life mission and divine purpose, helping to evoke the sort of energy that is magnetic to the people, opportunities and information that can help.

The best experience with this deck, or any of my oracle decks, will come when you slow down, connect with the breath and give yourself and the deck time to connect with each other and the Divine in sacred space. That could include lighting a candle and burning some incense, turning off your phone or other distracting devices and playing some nice, peaceful music, whilst you take some time, even if only briefly, to connect with your inner wisdom and the Divine.

It's helpful to treat communion with the cards as being something more special than just another thing to do during your day. This time is sacred communion with guiding wisdom. 'Sacred' means being able to go beyond the mundane, day-to-day world and open your heart and mind to your soul. That usually requires at least several deep, relaxing breaths and grounding your awareness out of your mind and into your body. You can do this through meditation or dance – or, if you are short on time, simply by placing your hand on your heart and mentally making the connection with your body as you prepare to receive soul guidance. It's about attitude and attention, about being present. When you do this, a short period of time can have proportionally huge returns on the rest of your day. And when those short time periods of sacred awareness happen regularly, they can shift the course of your life in extraordinary ways.

BLESSING THE DECK BEFORE FIRST USE

You may wish to bless the deck before using it for the first time. You may also wish to bless it again if you loan it to someone else to use. If you do readings for others using the deck, blessing it once is fine. Any time you feel that you need to strengthen and purify the energy of the deck, you can repeat the following simple blessing procedure. If you wish, you can do this before each reading, though it isn't strictly necessary. It is just about what feels best for you, what will support you to go deep into your own sacred connection with divine wisdom.

Here are the simple instructions for blessing the deck:

Hold the cards lightly against your chest, as though resting them over your heart. Say the following aloud with quiet confidence.

'The Divine loves unconditionally and flows through my heart, blessing me in entirety. The blessing extends into this deck, now. It becomes a divine voice of love, guidance, helpfulness and truth in my life and the lives of those all around me. I am grateful and open to receive such blessings with every use of this deck. So be it.'

The blessing is complete.

READINGS, SHUFFLING, REPEATED CARDS AND RANDOM CARDS FALLING OUT OF THE DECK

You can create your own simple readings using the layouts suggested below – or come up with your own layouts. Some people like to ask a specific question, such as those suggested below, then shuffle the deck and choose a card. They repeat that process for each question in the layout and then go back and read through each card message as they go, completing whichever healing process speaks to them most – whether that be all of them, or simply one or two that feel most resonant and relevant at the time.

Some people who are a little less patient (like myself!) like to shuffle thoroughly once and then simply pull out a card for each position in the layout. Actually, my favourite way to choose oracle cards – which has been my way for as long as I can remember – is just to ask a question and shuffle until a card flies out of the deck, which always seems to happen for me. However, if this method doesn't work for you that's perfectly okay. I mention it so that you know there really are no incorrect ways to choose cards. You'll always get what you need.

If you are aiming for the shuffle-and-falling-random-card technique, but end up with about half the deck falling out, rather than just one or two cards, then I suggest that you relax your energy. You may be a bit intense or overexcited and putting too much into your card deck! Relax. Shuffle, and even give yourself permission to fan out the cards face down on a table and choose one intuitively in that way, instead. It gives the energy in the deck a chance to calm down a little. Card readings generate energy, and keeping yourself calm and relaxed is a helpful way to get the intuitive hits from the reading that you need.

If you find that you are getting the same card repeatedly, don't feel bad – feel excited! There's a special significance in that card for you, and it's just being confirmed. If you are continuing to receive that message, it's not that you aren't getting it, it's that you are getting a deeper and deeper evolution of the message. This is sacred, and nothing to be concerned about. Ask to be shown the depth that your soul needs, as you re-visit the card message. Completing the healing process on numerous occasions for repeating card messages is highly recommended to help integrate the guidance.

HOW TO LAY OUT CARDS FOR READINGS WITH THIS DECK

Choose or adapt one of the simple rituals with card layout suggested – or create one of your own!

Place the cards in front of you. Place your left hand on the cards and say, 'Earth Mother and Heavenly Father, who love me unconditionally, I ask for a message of healing and guidance from you. I am open to what you wish to say now. Through divine grace and unconditional love, so be it.'

Then fan out the cards, or shuffle, according to your preference, laying out cards for the various positions below. Read the guidance for each card and do the healing process for as many, or as few, cards as feels intuitively right for you.

LAYOUT ONE:
EARTH MOTHER SPEAKS

Card One: What is the guidance from Mother Earth to enhance my physical life and wellbeing?

Card Two: What is the guidance from Mother Earth to enhance my emotional life and wellbeing?

Card Three: What is the guidance from Mother Earth to enhance my spiritual life and wellbeing?

Card Four: What is the guidance from Mother Earth about how I can give back to her most right now?

LAYOUT TWO:
LIFE-PURPOSE ADJUSTMENT WITH DIVINE GUIDANCE

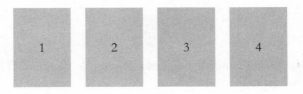

Card One: What qualities has my soul developed through past experiences that can most assist me now with my life purpose?

Card Two: What lessons am I learning at a soul level now that will most assist me in future with my life purpose?

Card Three: What guidance will help me stay on track, or get back on track, with my life purpose now?

Card Four: What divine guidance is there for my life purpose overall, now and in the future?

LAYOUT THREE:
A SIMPLE 'WHAT DO I MOST NEED TO KNOW NOW?' READING

This is a single-card layout for simple, focused guidance. It is my suggested go-to layout, unless you feel intuitively guided to work with one of the deeper layouts offered in this guidebook.

Card One: What do I most need to know at this time, for my highest good?

LAYOUT FOUR:
DIVINE HEALING AND SPIRITUAL GUIDANCE SESSION

This is for those moments when you may have either a specific question or an issue that you want to go deeper with – or when you want to perform a healing reading using the healing processes in the deck, along with a layout for a reading. If you don't have a specific question, you can still do this layout and benefit from it.

To begin, ask your question aloud. Keep it simple. If you have many questions, you will do better to ask one at a time, perhaps doing several readings over several days, as you allow clarity and guidance to come through.

If you don't have a specific question, or don't know how to even begin to formulate your questions, then you can simply ask, 'What is the best and most helpful higher guidance and healing for me now?'

Now, shuffle and choose the cards for each position in the layout, proceeding with the steps below.

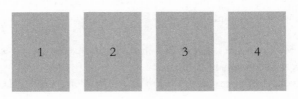

Card One: What is most helpful for me to focus upon at this time?

Read the initial opening paragraph for your card in the guidebook.

Place your hands on your heart and relax and breathe in that message for a few moments. Let the words soak deeper than your mind, into your heart and soul. Don't worry if they don't make sense to your logical mind right now. Let your mind relax as you contemplate the words and simply focus on your heart.

Card Two: What is the deeper soul guidance to bring me healing now?

Read the opening paragraph and main message for your card in the guidebook.

Reflect on this for a moment or two. Does it make sense to you? If not, that is okay. It means there is work going on for you at a soul level, deeper than your conscious mind has tapped into, as yet. This card is signalling that the mind can be open to what it doesn't yet understand and trust in the soul process.

When you are ready, complete the healing process for the card.

Card Three: What does my soul want me to know at this time?

Read the opening paragraph and main message. You have an option to complete the healing process for the card also, if that feels intuitively right for you.

Card Four: What is the most helpful guidance for me to receive now, to secure my best future?

Read the entire message for that card and complete the healing process.

When you have finished, say the following: 'Through divine grace, guidance and healing have been given. I trust in the presence of the Divine within my own soul to activate and empower my purpose, for the greatest good. May joy, fulfilment and divine will flow through my being now and always. So be it.'

Place your hands in prayer, or on your heart, whatever feels best for you, and simply be in connection with the divine love within you for a few moments.

If you can, take a few extra moments after this process to relax and focus on your breath, meditate or dance, or spend some time in nature, if you can, even if only for a short while.

Then simply return to your day or evening.

WHAT ARE THE HEALING PROCESSES?

The healing processes are simple, sacred rituals to help you integrate the wisdom of the card. Have you ever had an experience of really getting something at an intellectual level (like, 'I need to trust more! That makes everything easier for the Universe, and that includes me getting the help I need!'), only to find that you then fall back into old habits (such as worrying, instead of relaxing and having faith that what you need to successfully attain your purpose will come to you in the right way and at the right time)?

The healing processes help take the guidance of each card deeper than your mind, helping to integrate the message and frequency into your soul. You don't have to worry about whether they are working for you, or whether you understand why you are doing the process. It will work with your soul, and your soul has a way of being, of healing, of effecting change in your life and the world, which your mind will not often grasp until after it has happened. Then your mind may wonder how the change has actually come about! This is just the difference between the mind and the soul showing itself, and it's absolutely fine and wonderful. The healing processes help you connect with and trust in your soul, whilst giving your mind a process to follow to trigger these deeper integrations.

Now, go forth boldly and enjoy!

Card Messages

1. HO'ZHO
The Beauty Way of the Navajo

1. HO'ZHO
The Beauty Way of the Navajo

You are my sacred Earth Child, and I am your divine Earth Mother. With unconditional love, I provide all that you want and need so that you may fulfil your sacred destiny. We will always belong to each other. With abundance and generosity, I support you, revealing the divine beauty meant for you, so that joy and awe shall fill your soul. Relax now. It is time for you to be healed.

IN A READING

There is a beautiful solution available. Do not place your faith in worry or stress. Allow life to unfold. As you relax and give yourself permission to rest within the vastness and beauty of nature, you will become receptive to the best way to handle things. Don't try to figure it out by force. Let go and trust that what is needed is coming to you at the perfect time and in the perfect way. Your peaceful mind shall perceive readily and accurately all that you need to know.

SPIRITUAL GUIDANCE

The Beauty Way reminds you that beneath the noise, beneath your worries and concerns, there is oneness between you and life. Even if your world may feel chaotic at times, even if you fear that you have gone off track, the path that will return you to peace, beauty, balance and harmony is always here for you. You do not have to become stressed or exhausted to fix what isn't working. Solutions can come to you more easily when you allow yourself to drop out of the pain and into the pleasure of the Beauty Way. Sometimes, problems will disappear altogether in this place, and you shall realise that they were nothing more than the dark creation of an overworked, fatigued mind. Sometimes, you will discover a different way to look at things, a helpful vision gifted by Great Spirit, and gain the energy to become productive, applying a simple and inspired idea that changes everything.

The Beauty Way isn't about ignoring the reality of the world or becoming superficial. The Beauty Way is a deep spiritual feeling of trust, openness, and appreciation of the divine presence shining in all aspects of life. This appreciation restores the soul with a sublime recognition of a greater, loving intelligence that is always present, always inviting, always responding. When some form of ugliness is disturbing your soul, threatening to steal your peaceful trust in the Divine, you are guided to come back to the Beauty Way, back into worshipful reverence of the sacred. From that place, you then become empowered to deal with the situation in a way that increases love and joy in yourself and the world. Rather than being overtaken by the ugliness, you are able to offer beauty instead.

Can you relax for a moment now? This is your first step into the Beauty Way. Allow the simple beauty of nature, of human kindness, of divine love to seep deep into your soul, infusing it like a sacred tea. Divine beauty moves through you and fills you, bringing you a lightly euphoric feeling. You can be uplifted. Renewed. At peace. The Divine Feminine knows how to create beautiful harmony. She includes you, your life journey, all human beings and the world as a whole within her wisdom and grace. When you relax into her beauty, she will show you many possibilities. She will help you attract what you need and want most. In this way, you can become a channel through which her creative healing energy can flow abundantly into your life and to others in this world.

HEALING PROCESS
Holding the card lightly at your heart and the guidebook comfortably in your other hand, say the following aloud:

Today I walk the Beauty Way,
All darkness and evil departs.
I now become beauty and peace,
With the cool breeze of divine grace renewing me from within.
My thoughts and my words are beautiful.
Nothing shall hinder my reverence and ease.
All day I walk the Beauty Way.

Turn to the east (or your right). Say aloud: *The children of the earth are beautiful and blessed with wisdom. Care is given for all beings of the earth that are vulnerable and in need of divine protection. They play in divine beauty.*

Turn to the south (or turn again to your right). Say aloud: *The young people of the earth are beautiful and blessed with wisdom. The flow of life energy is aligned with divine will to benefit all, for the greatest good. They dance in divine beauty.*

Turn to the west (or turn again to your right). Say aloud: *The parents of the earth are beautiful and blessed with wisdom. Spiritual strength and true guardianship of all earth's beings prevail. They love in divine beauty.*

Turn to the North (or turn again to your right). Say aloud: *The grandparents of the earth are beautiful and blessed with wisdom. Guidance is given and heeded to create harmony, peace and beauty between all peoples and the earth. They rest in divine beauty.*

Standing in the centre, say the following aloud:

I walk with beauty before me. I walk with beauty behind me.
I walk with beauty below me. I walk with beauty above me.
I walk with beauty all around me and within every part of my soul.

Take a moment to feel connection to your heart. Believe in the power of your words. Feel what it is like to trust in the healing divine beauty that flows in you and throughout all of life.

You have completed your healing process.

2. ESTANATLEHI

Turquoise Changing Woman

2. ESTANATLEHI
Turquoise Changing Woman

I am the Turquoise Moon Mother, and I come to you now with a message of change. This may be change that you want or change that you fear, but either way, I will show you how to use this change to become stronger, wiser and more empowered to fulfil your divine destiny. Do not fear the changes around you and within you. Trust in the timing of what is happening in your world.

IN A READING

Change is upon you. It is essential for your continued growth, and you do not need to fear it. As you allow for this change, remain steadfast in your inner spiritual connection. This gives you courage, trust, peace and reassurance, and you will find ways to navigate the shift so that your life improves through the process. If you are thinking of making a change, you are encouraged to do so without trying to force it. Be open and do your part to the best of your ability – but also tune in to your sense of divine timing, asking the Universe for help and allowing life to unfold according to its own rhythm of creative, loving intelligence.

SPIRITUAL GUIDANCE

Estanatlehi (pronounced es-tan-AHT-lu-hee) is the Turquoise Moon Goddess of the Navajo, known as Changing Woman. She is always changing and yet never dies. As she begins to age she simply turns to walk to the east, the direction of the rising sun and beginnings, where she is renewed. Her blessings are for nourishment, renewal of energy and new beginnings. She brings hope, and reminds us that life is constantly renewing itself around us and within us. We can always begin again in that spirit of renewal. In the face of loss or destruction, her presence brings comfort, hope and peace, so that rather than losing faith and giving up because we feel defeated, we have the courage to continue to fight for what matters – with refreshed reserves of energy and enthusiasm.

If we are struggling with change – either too much of it or perhaps too little of it – Estanatlehi comes to us with reassuring guidance. When something is in need of repair, Great Spirit knows how to restore it. When something needs to end, Great Spirit will show the way to empty ourselves of the past and prepare for a new beginning. When there is lack or deprivation, the abundance and generosity of the Universe shall bring fullness. We do not need to fear change, whether wanted or unwanted. We just need to trust in the good and loving workings of the Universe. Estanatlehi reminds us of the divine feminine wisdom and power which expresses itself as life, always flowing, always changing, always evolving. We belong to life and can trust in it. Evolution is not always easy – often it requires tremendous courage of heart and inner strength. Yet the Turquoise Moon Mother will help us respond to any change in a way that increases love, light and wisdom within us and the world.

Turquoise Changing Woman is also known as the conqueror of monsters and the bringer of blessings, especially when we feel that we are under attack or lacking something that we need.

She teaches us that it is safe to rest our unconditional faith in divine grace. We make our efforts as wholeheartedly as we can – but in the gap between what we can do and what needs to be accomplished for beauty, peace and healing to happen on this planet, divine grace is there as the bridge, the catalyst, the miracle-worker. Grace does not do the work for us, but it does empower our efforts and assist us in fulfilling our purpose in ways the mind can rarely anticipate. Grace is the invisible and empowering hand of Great Spirit reaching for us daily. Turquoise Moon Mother watches over us with a reminder that we are not in this alone, that the Divine is our creative partner in all pursuits. We only need ask for help to be given, to realise that it is already there, waiting for us to receive it.

HEALING PROCESS
Find a comfortable place to sit quietly.

Say aloud: *Through unconditional love, I am blessed and empowered to grow through change. All that I need to evolve into the next expression of my divine destiny is generously provided for me. I surrender into divine blessing for renewal, now, open to receive my highest good. So be it.*

Hold the card and gaze at the moon behind the goddess. Reflect upon her image and the way her left thumb gently brings focus to her forehead, and, with her right palm facing upwards, she reaches to the ground beneath her. Here she bestows blessings.

Take a moment to centre yourself in your heart. Are you open and willing to receive a divine blessing? Can you allow yourself to become clear and receptive, trusting in what will be granted?

When you are ready, you may wish to mirror the pose depicted in the card image by placing your own left thumb on your forehead for a few moments as you extend your right arm out, palm facing upwards. You don't have to think – all you need to do is breathe and be, as though divine blessing is flowing through you from the Divine Mother and into the world.

Allow your gaze to become soft and diffuse, and when you are ready, close your eyes and relax. Stay in that relaxed state for as long as feels right for you. You may wish to chant, to meditate or even to fall asleep. When you are ready, awaken and ground yourself with some physical movement.

You have completed your healing process.

3. TOTEMIC PUMA
Power Awakening

3. TOTEMIC PUMA

Power Awakening

I am Puma. I awaken within you the vigorous energy, fierce power and ability to act without hesitation when the moment is right. My patience and strategy, my preparation and precision, my fearlessness and decisiveness are now your own. Allow my sacred medicine to fill your soul and bring courage to your heart. You have come into your power.

IN A READING

You've got this. Don't let fear or hesitation hold you back. Apply yourself fully to the task. Let go of old ways of viewing yourself as incapable, scattered or wasteful of energy. You have the ability to focus intently, to generate clear intention, and to achieve your ambitions through methodical steps and an applied will. You have the internal resources you need for successful completion. Even if no one else recognises your potential and believes in your future success, in due course they will understand differently. By then, you will already be moving on to your next task. Trust your sense of timing. Have patience. When you know it is the time to leap, do it without hesitation.

SPIRITUAL GUIDANCE

Puma moves through your soul as guardian and guide. When Puma appears, it is a significant sign that you have come into your power. Puma moves with stealth and silence. Observing, being patient as she narrows her focus, she cultivates energy so that the correct amount of inner power for the outer action is there when needed. When she strikes, it is with precision and effectiveness. She doesn't waste energy. She chooses her opportunities. Hesitation is not in her nature. There is no time or energy for doubt and uncertainty when one is fully engaged in conscious participation in the moment.

You may wonder if this sounds much like you. You may consider yourself to be – at least sometimes – more of a doubter than one prone to fearlessness and certainty. Yet the soul medicine of Puma builds within us silently. We may not even realise that her power is there, until all of a sudden, when it is needed, we act with unerring focus and unwavering commitment. We literally 'didn't know we had it in us' until the time came and an attitude of swift, unfailing responsiveness somehow rose up from within.

Puma moves with stealth until the right moment to act is upon her. Then she leaves her cover behind and, with unwavering focus, she strikes. You are guided by her to keep your motives, plans and preparation out of public view. Attend to your work. Become ready to be it, rather than talk about it.

Part of this medicine is strategy. Planning. Visualising the end result. This requires simplicity and clarity. Even if the destiny you are seeking to manifest is big and bold, there will still be simple steps to take along the way. Puma is the huntress with singular focus. She goes after what is required in that moment, one step at a time, and thereby attains her goals. She strikes successfully because she works precisely. Take time to formulate your goals, and go after them one by one, with a sense of patience and calculated timing. Take charge of the situation by your willingness to be patient, to bide your time, to cultivate energy and courage – and trust your intuition to leap when you know the right moment is upon you.

Puma might bring us the power we need to step up into a new role, seize control of a failing project, cut off a toxic situation in our lives or cease unhelpful negative self-talk in our own mind. She indicates that a changing relationship with power is available to you now. If you have been repelled by negative uses of power by others, or even yourself, recognise this and let it go. Forgive. Give yourself the chance to open up to using your power in a safe and wise way. Know that you are smart enough to learn from what didn't honour your soul in the past. When you ask for Great Spirit to guide you from within your heart, your movements in the world shall benefit more than only yourself. This right use of power – surrendered and in service to the great power of the Divine – will help you overcome your reluctance and lay claim to your will. You need your will to transform inspiration into action. The world truly needs this from you. Whatever it is that you dream of attaining or desire to do in this world, Puma arrives with this message – *you have the power.*

HEALING PROCESS
Find a comfortable place to relax.

Say aloud: *Puma, spirit of the sun, fire of the earth, you are fierceness and intelligent use of power, embodied in sacred feminine form. Your presence awakens the power within my soul, and I leave doubt and fear behind. I am patient. I am determined. I shall not be swayed from my purpose. Procrastination and hesitation are no longer part of my way. I embrace your gifts for the greatest good.*

With your certainty, I find my own conviction renewed. It is not a question of if, but a question of when. My spiritual attainment is inevitable. So be it.

Read through this simple visualisation slowly, as you feel the energy in the description:

Golden fur shimmering copper in the sunlight. Heat pulsing beneath the skin, as waves of contained energy are ready to be channelled in clean action at the right moment. Lean and powerful muscle. Watchful steady gaze, no thought or distraction, just pure focus. The power rises within, and the moment to leap is here. Action! Aliveness! This medicine wisdom of bold aliveness without hesitation is within my own soul, and I claim it.

Now, either close your eyes and relax, or get up and move your body in whatever way feels best, for as long as feels good for you.

You have completed your healing process.

4. GODDESS OF TEOTIHUACAN

She Guards the Waters of Life

The ancient guardian mother protects the waters of life and offers her protection and blessing. Her appearance augurs a time of purification and cleansing, leading to enhanced fertility. You are a creator of new consciousness, a generator of positive energy as fuel for constructive outcomes. We need your vitalised being to keep nourishing the human collective with helpful alternatives to mainstream consciousness. You will be protected and supported at the deep level of soul in order to become the creator and custodian of a clean reservoir of consciousness from which souls, thirsty for purity, relief and love, can drink. The ancient mother will help you to help her and the many creatures within her care. She will help you to be fearlessly inventive with your loving creations of healing consciousness.

IN A READING

Consider very seriously the need to cut cords to negative or unhelpful influences in your life – whether they be habits, people or forms of entertainment and media that threaten to distort the pure and wise use of your wild spirit and ignited mind! Whilst it is important that you engage with others, the sacred creator within you requires time and space in solitude to process, reflect, contemplate and create. Only then can you remember who you are and what is important to you – and summon the inner power to act accordingly. In that way, you will not become overly swayed by any lesser force, particularly mainstream consciousness that perpetuates victimising thought patterns and behaviours. Give yourself a chance for spiritual, psychological and emotional time out and cleansing so that you can recognise the inner truth of your own soul and adhere to it faithfully.

SPIRITUAL GUIDANCE

Sacred Mother has come to you in honour of the important work you have to accomplish as a creator of consciousness, a free thinker and a seeker of truth. What original healing stories will you give birth to in your life and this world? If you've become dried up and depleted, the Divine Mother brings you nourishment. Let the inner well of your soul be filled with her presence and grace through deep rest and contemplation. Give yourself space and time for renewal, and allow any overload of mind or nervous system to discharge into earth. If you have lost the zest for your passion, or have become confused or overwhelmed, scattered with too many ideas or directions, you are in need of the spiritual cleansing which her blessing brings to you.

The waters of your own consciousness must be safeguarded so that they can become a tonic for the souls of others. When you highly value your uniqueness and originality, you become willing to bear the uncertainty that accompanies absence of the familiar. Vigorously contest any who attempt to exploit, direct or distort the true expression of your higher knowing. In contemplation, impure material separates from the truth and is filtered out of the soul. The purity of your truth – such a seemingly subtle quality – has an astonishing power to effect change. As you take time to allow purity to emerge from deeply restful, reflective meditation, your personal energy and spiritual potency grow. Your potential to be an influence in this world increases accordingly. However, so too does the interest of less noble creatures in exploiting that delicious divine power for their own nefarious purpose! Avoid such tragedy by refusing to entertain any person or idea that drains, depletes or diminishes the quality of your consciousness. Be resolute and exacting. If it's not right, courageously and unapologetically cast it out.

In your uncompromising defence of your most strange and beautiful ideas, uplifting truth and fierce loving wisdom, you will come to know what it feels like to be as a new world in and of yourself. You will feel your being like a planet in devotional orbit around a divine sun. Instead of contorting yourself to fit into the frustrated and grasping world of others, you will offer those seeking something more beautiful the opportunity of finding refuge within your world. Instead of being influenced, you become an influencer. Instead of trying to dominate others, you awaken within them the desire for their own higher nature. You effect healing transformation without force. This is the way of yin power, of the sacred water wisdom that cleanses the impure and creates new life without diminishing its life force.

You have the opportunity to shift from stressful striving to more restful and abundant creation, sourced from the depths of your being in silent, absorbing communion with the Divine. It takes discipline and commitment to learn this new way of being, to recognise the essential need for time and space in contemplation to consciously create. It takes courage to refuse to bow down to the productivity pushers, who aren't interested in authentic offerings that heal both through the process of their creation as well as in their final form. Instead, they just want more stuff to perpetuate conveyer-belt consumerism for the genuine benefit of no one. Your refusals are sacred. They bring with them the thirst-quenching waters of grace, bestowing freedom, wellbeing and soul-satisfying experiences of fulfilment.

HEALING PROCESS

Say aloud: *Divine Mother, please help humankind to understand and implement the best ways to protect the natural resources of this planet. May we use the creative power of our consciousness with wild loving reverence for life, generating wise action and purifying the waters of spiritual grace to restore all beings thirsty for truth.*

When you are ready, you may like to drink some clean, pure water with gratitude. Imagine as you do so a world where all living beings have access to clean pure water, where the oceans are clean and pure, and the rivers are clean and pure. Let yourself feel joy and gratitude with such a visualisation. All reality begins with consciousness. Let us use every opportunity we can to support the necessary shift for life to thrive.

You have completed your healing process.

5. CIRCLE CROSS OF TENAN

Rare Intersection of Heaven and Earth

5. CIRCLE CROSS OF TENAN
Rare Intersection of Heaven and Earth

Your plans and purpose are in alignment with greater cosmic forces. Whether you see it coming or not, things will fall into place and what you have been working towards will come to fruition. A rare intersection of heaven and earth will result in a precious manifestation of grace. The Divine shall correct a situation that is in need of realignment. Fear not. Pray boldly and be faithful. All is well.

IN A READING

Your soul is a facilitator of sacred union between the spiritual realms and the earthly world. Whether you do this as an artist, a healer, an activist, a priestess or shaman or in some other way, honour your path and your purpose. Take care of yourself and prioritise your spiritual life according to the practices and methods that help you remain open, connected and grounded, with your heart open to Great Spirit and moved by love for our earth. You are part of a team of souls working to keep the balance of light on our planet intact, accessible and vital. Offer yourself to the divine plan, without holding anything back – and know that you shall be helped in countless ways, just as you offer your own will and talent to the sacred purpose of healing in this world.

SPIRITUAL GUIDANCE

There are times when heaven and earth align and the power unleashed is considerable. People rally and situations fall into place. As if by a miracle, patience, persistence, effort and energy finally come together and a creation of tangible goodness takes shape in the world. It can be unexpected. You may even have almost given up hope. Then, suddenly, everything comes together. The Circle Cross of Tenan is a sign of such a happening in your world, a moment of powerful grace, where Spirit makes its presence felt upon the earth.

The hawk is typically a solar creature, thriving in the light, and yet there are some hawks that are able to hunt by night. You, like the rare lunar hawk, are one who is of the light, yet can move through the darkness successfully. You have enough spiritual light within you to be able to see your way through lies and deception and find the truth that you seek. What you are seeking is meant to be yours by divine right. Keep up the process of growth and enquiry, and it will come to you at the right moment, according to higher spiritual law, through the operation of spiritual grace.

The priestess, the one who bridges heaven and earth, dwells within the lunar pyramid of the ancient city of Teotihuacan, known as Tenan, with the circle crosses as her guide. She intuitively knows when and how to call for heavenly assistance, as all priestesses do. Part of her role is prayer for those in her spiritual care, invoking divine love and requesting heavenly assistance and grace for all living beings. This is her spiritual responsibility – to keep the channels between heaven and earth not only open, but healthy and robust, active and stable. Why? Because she is capable of doing so. This is your sacred role, also. Pray to the unconditionally loving divine source for all events, for all beings. Take active steps to fulfil your destiny and be the living channel for spiritual grace that you are destined to be.

HEALING PROCESS
You can create your own circle cross or gaze at the image below. If you wish to create your own, you can do this with small crystals, with rope or scarves, with candles or by drawing it on paper and creating a sacred piece of art. You may want to dance your circle cross, or sing it into being too.

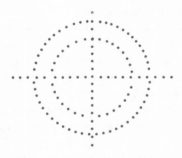

The circle cross is the symbol of the portal between heaven and earth that exists within your own soul. As you create your circle cross, or simply gaze at the image, know that heaven and earth are connecting with each other through your own soul.

Turn to the east (or your right) and say: *Through the protective gateway of unconditional love, I invite the power of divine grace into my being and into this world.*

Turn to the south (or turn again to your right) and say aloud:

Through the protective gateway of unconditional love, I invite the power of divine will into my being and into this world.

Turn to the west (or turn again to your right) and say aloud: *Through the protective gateway of unconditional love, I invite the power of divine healing into my being and into this world.*

Turn to the north (or turn again to your right and say aloud: *Through the protective gateway of unconditional love, I invite the power of divine presence into my being and into this world.*

Put your attention on the ground beneath your feet and say aloud: *Earth Mother, may all of humanity love, honour and protect you. Thank you for all that you do for us. You are a Buddha Mother of creativity, generosity and wild grace.*

Put your attention on the sky above your head and say aloud: *On behalf of all humanity, I invoke divine love, light and wisdom for the fulfilment of purpose for all divine beings. May we be assisted through the endless divine resource for the greatest good for all generations. May divine grace evoke love and higher consciousness in all realms. It is done.*

Place your hands in prayer for a moment. Relax.

You have completed your healing process.

6. PALHIK MANA
Medicine of the Butterfly Kachina

6. PALHIK MANA
Medicine of the Butterfly Kachina

On wings of hope, Butterfly Kachina guides you through an ending to the light of new life within. It is your transition into a happier time, of increased pleasure and delight. Especially if you have experienced great struggle or loss, the spirit medicine of Butterfly brings hopeful promise to your heart. Here is your sign that there will be happiness, peace and light. Trust in the goodness being birthed.

IN A READING

An apparently lost cause or shattered dream was a necessary part of your transformational journey. What was sacrificed can be reborn into something even more beautiful. You are not meant to turn to the past, as it cannot support you in the way it once did. Trust that you have the inner resources to handle what is happening within you and in your life. You are moving towards a significant psychological, emotional and perhaps also physical breakthrough and transformation. You may have an inner sense of discomfort signalling that something new is unfolding within. It is natural to initially feel a little awkward or uncertain in the face of the unfamiliar. This is a good sign of change stirring from within. Allow nature to take its course. Trust in what is happening, even whilst you don't fully understand it. It will turn out beautifully in the end (which will also happen to be a new beginning).

SPIRITUAL GUIDANCE

There are moments when even those of us with great courage feel tested beyond our faith. Doubt, darkness and despair can creep into our minds and lash our hearts with fear. Perhaps there seems to be good reason for our pain – the loss of a loved one, a cherished hope dashed, disturbing human behaviour, the state of the environment or some other unexpected and painful shock. There may be no particular reason for it, and yet we are somehow gripped by feelings of anxiety or despair that we cannot resolve, no matter how hard we try.

The healing soul medicine of the Butterfly Kachina comes to you now to alleviate your suffering, to remind you that everything you have gone through has been part of what has made you strong, compassionate and wise. When all seems lost – perhaps especially then – our soul needs the gift of seeing the light, love and wisdom of Great Spirit at work behind all things, at all times, always reaching out to us and always offering love. The soul needs faith and hope like the body needs air to breathe. Faith keeps the soul alive and well.

You do not have to regret anything that has happened. You do not have to judge yourself or any other, or wish that things had been different. You have not missed out. You have not messed up. You have been learning and growing. What is required from you now is a willingness to let it fall away, because the person you once were actually no longer exists. You may not fully realise it yet. Like the butterfly trying to crawl on the ground like a caterpillar, you may mourn the loss of your old caterpillar ways. Yet, if you take a moment to witness yourself anew now, you'll realise you are not the person from two years or ten years ago. You can then open to the gifts that Butterfly Kachina is bringing to you now – wellbeing, new life, vibrancy, freedom and happiness.

If you have been working hard on an issue, on yourself or on a cause in the world, and it seems to be going nowhere, Butterfly Kachina reminds you that in the divine alchemy of transformation things sometimes appear to be going backwards as they move forward. It is the way of things. After summer there is autumn and then winter, all of which indicate progress towards the next spring. If you didn't understand the creative purpose and regenerative nature of the seasons, you might be frightened by the winter, concerned that it signified the world was ending! With knowledge of the sacred feminine wisdom of the seasons, you are not afraid of winter – you see it as an essential part of life. You may even learn to nurture and restore yourself during that time, gaining conscious benefit and appreciation for it. If you feel you are in a spiritual or emotional winter in your life, have hope. The soul unfolds according to seasons just as nature does. Let your heart and mind rest in trust that life is growing your soul into its beautiful fulfilment.

HEALING PROCESS

Butterfly takes us out of seriousness and into childlike joy. Is there something that you used to love to do as a child? Is there some activity that makes you feel healthily childlike – perhaps laughing at funny animal videos or going for a walk in nature? Colouring in or pulling a hula hoop out of the back of the wardrobe? Playing drums on the pots and pans? Singing and dancing in your lounge room? Take some time to be with your inner child self and be engaged completely in the present moment.

When you are ready, say this prayer aloud: *I give thanks for the sacred soul medicine of the Butterfly Kachina, to the ever-renewing power of life. I honour all that I have been through, for it has brought me to this moment. Now, I am strong, wise, compassionate and empowered. I accept life, and I am ready for the rebirth that is happening now in my own soul and in the world. May divine love support successful transitions for our world. May all beings move into love, freedom, peace and happiness. I embrace this moment. So be it.*

You have completed your healing process.

7. LINÁ
Wat Must Be, Shall Be

7. LINÁ

What Must Be, Shall Be

You have beautiful dreams and inspired, bold ambitions. You are guided to believe that they are a natural expression of your soul, something that is meant to be. Life will support you in the expression of those dreams and ambitions, even in the moments where it seems to be struggle, rather than support, that you are experiencing. The process for transformation into full maturity involves learning how to grow through light and through darkness back to the light again. You will always find your way back to the light. Have faith in yourself and what must be. Dedicate yourself to what you love without hesitation.

IN A READING

If you are experiencing loss or change, have faith. Sometimes things happen that seem to be working against us. It is only later that they show themselves to have been valuable ways by which we acquired the greater faith, courage and determination that were necessary to the fulfilment of our purpose. Know that your destiny is unfolding, and you are moving through circumstances that are ultimately going to help you become your soul in fullness and splendour. Keep going. Everything happening in your life is helping you to fulfil your divine potential. Know that any darkness will give way to the light.

SPIRITUAL GUIDANCE

Just as life and death are natural, so too is growth. It is natural for the caterpillar to become the butterfly. It is extraordinary to the point of being almost unbelievable, if we were to really think about it, but natural nonetheless. It is natural for the bones of the sacred cow to return to the earth, to give her minerals which, in turn, support new life. So, it is meant to be that with human life there is loss that becomes part of what allows for something new to be vitalised. You are here to grow into all that you are. You are here to bring certain dreams to life in this world. They are meant to be healing dreams for a new world, because that is your nature, your innate soul way. Just like the seemingly impossible journey of the butterfly, with sacred endings that support new beginnings, you too are moving through the cycle of life.

Sometimes this can be confronting. To give up old ways or old identities can seem frightening to the mind. Yet it is inspiring and exciting for the soul that yearns to blossom into fullness and cannot thrive when it is held back in fear. You may forget this momentarily and turn back from where you are headed out of confusion or concern. It may seem as though you are being asked to give up too much to secure your goals – or you may wonder if it is foolish imagination, rather than genuine soul purpose, that is driving you forward. If you are a visionary with ideas that are not yet widely understood, but will help push humanity towards the new world, you may struggle more than most. In this case, you are asked to take leaps of faith and endure the endings inherent in evolution whilst waiting for the signs of new life. You will have this asked of you because it is necessary for the process of creation and, most importantly, for you to have enough faith in your soul to handle it.

To have faith in your own purpose when it may sometimes feel like you are fighting a losing battle takes a lot of heart. Great Spirit knows what you are up to, and it wants to remind you that you are not being foolish – you are following your destiny. Great Spirit wants you to accept that it can help you, that what you are pursuing is meant to be, and as you keep to your course, success will come. Allow the inner force that compels you forward to have its way. Do not fear the sometimes radical changes that take place as you evolve into your destiny. Any losses or endings along the way are essential for your fulfilment. Let your trust in life's good will and generous support of you be unconditional. Know you shall thrive.

HEALING PROCESS

Say this prayer aloud: *I call upon the wild grace of the Sacred Feminine, and give gratitude for your wise and loving assistance in my life. I accept your blessing to fulfil myself. I trust that you will show me the signs and impress upon me the guidance that I need so as to feel reassured, focused and committed. Help me and all beings fulfil the plan that Great Spirit intends for us and has placed in our hearts. Only the goodness of your wisdom prevails, and every darkness leads me into greater light. So be it.*

If you can spend a little time reflecting in nature, do that. It can help you remember the cycle of life and have faith that the earth knows how to support life with brilliance and care.

Finish with this short prayer to your own soul: *My dear soul, you know what you are doing and how to grow in harmony with divine genius and sacred purpose, even when my conscious mind does not understand. You know, when I do not know. So I choose to trust you. And this brings me peace and comfort now. I trust you.*

Place your hands in prayer at your heart and bow your head. Allow yourself to sense, feel or intend to recognise the unlimited expressions of love from Great Spirit for you. It emanates all around you, towards you in all directions and shines from within you, outwards in all directions. So much love, support and light is bringing comfort and reassurance to you now.

You have completed your healing process.

8. ULUKA VAHINI

She Who Rides the Owl Brings Justice

8. ULUKA VAHINI
She Who Rides the Owl Brings Justice

I am the goddess of karma, wealth and balance. I come to correct adharma, that which is dark, unnatural and against nature, life, love and goodness. I redress the misuse of wealth and power. I enact divine justice and restore divine order. Trust in the innocence of your own soul and fear not, for I am ever watchful, and my power brings truth. Divine justice is always brought to bear.

IN A READING

Don't waste your valuable time and energy worrying about people getting away with things. It's not possible. Everything is balanced out by karma in the long run. If you feel down or depressed, take action immediately to reconnect to joy, healing energy and vitality of spirit. All things are measured and metered by clear divine vision, and your job is to put your faith in the work of the Divine, whilst you tend to your own journey with trust and commitment.

SPIRITUAL GUIDANCE

From the perspective of those with awakened hearts, the world can sometimes appear to be a disturbing and frightening place where negative activity leads to prosperity, whilst good and worthy people struggle and suffer. It may appear that those who have wisdom are barely heard, whilst angry people with fear in their heart are afforded attention and power. It may seem that what matters most is tended to the least, whilst destructive purposes gain mass support, and constructive causes struggle to maintain existence. It is very easy, with such a view of things, for the pure of heart to become angry, bitter and despairing.

However, you are meant to be a light in this world, and it is important that you allow Great Spirit to support you in this task. Safeguarding your state of mind is essential for you to accomplish your life purpose. If you get caught up in negative thinking – as may happen from time to time – allow Great Spirit to guide you back to the truth of your inner light. Remember that the Divine is more powerful than any nightmare created by human darkness. You don't have to deny the dark side of human nature or its manifest consequences for the health of the planet, but you do need to keep yourself secure within the light so that you can effectively fulfil your destiny as an Earth Warrior. Joy, happiness and peace will not diminish your motivation to serve love. Rather, they will ensure you have enough energy to do so effectively.

Whether you are facing a sense of injustice in your personal life, or feel despair at the choices humanity is making in a broader sense, know that the Divine has a grander plan than we can possibly understand. We are here to fight for love and do all that we can to honour what is true for us. We are meant to call upon the Universe for assistance in all ways possible. We are meant to use our strengths of love, compassion, wisdom, light and kindness to be kick-ass Earth Warriors who will never give up, who are smart enough to use every resource they can – including their living connection to Great Spirit – to affirm correct priorities that honour life. In this way, we uplift ourselves and inspire others through our life journey.

There are dark forces that want you to lose hope, because they know that when your heart is hopeful, you are unstoppable. Trust that the Divine will take care of the darkness. Trust that karmic forces will balance the scales of higher justice with unerring accuracy – whilst you do everything in your power to remain connected to the light, as you bring your loving energy, purpose and passion to the world.

HEALING PROCESS

Repeat this prayer aloud three times: *Through unconditional divine love and my own free will, I surrender that which is not rightfully mine.*

Bow your head and open your hands, palms facing up. Allow this to feel like a position of surrender and vulnerability. You may like to imagine or pretend that you are releasing old energy out of your hands and it is gently dripping into the earth where it can be naturally transformed by the Earth Mother's alchemical power. Take a few moments here.

Don't be afraid to let go. Remember that you could be unintentionally holding on to things that you don't even want. Or, you could be holding on to things that you think you want and need but that are actually getting in the way of you receiving what will be amazing, helpful, wonderful and perfect for you in all ways.

When you are ready, raise your head and hands back to a comfortable position.

Say aloud: *Love can conquer anything, even karma. Through divine grace and mercy, I call upon unconditional love to cleanse, purify and assist me now in all ways. May divine love flow through me to manifest the will of Great Spirit in the world. May all beings who have become lost in darkness be mercifully guided back into the light of divine love through the grace of Great Spirit. So be it.*

Place your hands in front of your heart, with the palms facing up as if to receive. Keep your hands softly there and close your eyes, as you chant or say aloud: *The divine blesses me. I am filled and blessed. Repeat this statement as many times as feels good for you.*

Relax for a few moments, feeling gratitude and fullness of heart.

You have completed your healing process.

9. BLESSING OF KUMU
No Good Thing Shall Be Withheld

9. BLESSING OF KUMU
No Good Thing Shall Be Withheld

The Universe wants to express its creativity, healing and brilliance through you. It does not want to be limited to repeating what has already been. Newness needs to burst through you into startling expressions of abundant life. You are guided into unknown territory, guided to go beyond that which you have known yourself and your world to be, so that something original and necessary can be brought to life. The Universe knows all that you are in need of so that you can best attain your destiny. All shall be provided for you. Expand your faith to allow for the greater workings of Great Spirit.

IN A READING

Resources are coming to you now. If you have been in lack, limitation or anxiety about such things happening, relax and substitute your stress for absolute trust that the Universe will provide all good things with generosity and grace. If you find this challenging, take it one step at a time, reprogramming your heart and mind into new habits of peaceful trust. It will feel much better to live like this. It is not foolishness but wisdom that embraces such unconditional faith. Know that the provision of all resources required is a certainty. The only variables are the details of how the journey unfolds. When you tune into your heart, you'll remember that you are loved, protected and guided in every moment. Trust the Universe.

SPIRITUAL GUIDANCE

When you are a dreamer, a visionary and a seer of the need for transformation in our world, it can be easy to feel intimidated, to dismiss the possibility for radical change as unrealistic, to believe that the greatest of our visions are unattainable in the real world. However, many things that were once considered to be impossible to the human mind are now part of our daily lives. The impossible becomes possible on a regular basis.

Kumu is the Hawaiian term for teacher and source of wisdom. The Universe is the great kumu. When we trust in the Universe, we come to understand certain truths, including the realisation that we don't have to be limited to what we logically know. If we are willing to expand our faith, then that which we are capable of experiencing in harmony with the Universe will expand, also.

Your beautiful and perhaps impossible-seeming dreams are supported by the unlimited resources of the Universe. Even if you don't know what is needed – and when – in order to create a successful outcome, the Universe does. You are being guided to re-set your mind and heart to unconditional trust. This can be a challenge for the human part of us that tends to give weight mostly to what can be perceived through the five bodily senses – yet, for your spirit, this is easy. The spirit within you knows the incredible power of the Divine to bring together all aspects of life in the perfect way, at the perfect time, for astounding success. Your spirit knows that when you take action on your most apparently impossible divine mission from a position of faith rather than a more limited perspective, the Universe helps you every step of the way.

It is time to adjust your belief systems to encompass this

entire Universe as your creative partner in life. It provides you with resources, opportunities and learning experiences to gain precious information and life skills so that you are singularly and completely equipped to do what you have come to this planet to do. Kumu, the great wisdom teacher, guides you now. Don't allow your mind to create visions of poverty or lack, of failure or absence of support. Focus instead upon the sweet generosity of the Universe lovingly providing for you – often in advance of you consciously realising what you need – with all that is necessary for your best life and fulfilment of your sacred purpose. All the answers, the connections, the resources, everything that you need is right there for you at the best moment.

With a focus on a feeling of excitement about opportunities, inspirational innovation and the best and brightest of human creative endeavour, surge forward in harmony with each other to establish sustainable new systems. You can lend your energy, your mind and your body to what you want to have happen in this world. The Universe will hear and feel you and provide resources accordingly. Let your thoughts and hopes become your prayers, and the answers to those prayers will benefit all life on this planet.

HEALING PROCESS

Say this prayer aloud: *I am so grateful for the generosity, abundance and attentiveness of the Universe to my needs. I am provided for with such grace and love. All resources for my life purpose to be successfully and joyfully expressed are freely given to me. May all beings consciously know the loving embrace of the Universe and fulfil their sacred purpose. So be it.*

Write or consider a list of at least five things that you are grateful for. They might be simple things that have happened today or experiences from your past. If you can recall a time where you felt the Universe stepped into help you out, and it was an unexpected and very welcome blessing, list that, too. Read your list aloud. Allow this list to reinforce your sense of trust and wonder in the kindness and protection of the Universe towards you.

Relax for a moment with your hands in prayer at your heart. Imagine that the generous, wise, loving and joyful universal energy is overflowing within your heart.

You've completed your healing process.

10. KAITIAKI

Guardian of Papatūānuku

10. KAITIAKI
Guardian of Papatūānuku

You are Kaitiaki, guardian of the Divine Feminine. Your relationship with Mother Earth, Papatūānuku, is sacred, empowering and healing. You are destined to become more spiritually intimate with her, sharing in her creative potency and wisdom. Lean into her and trust in her support, even as you serve her by courageously voicing truth. She is your great ally, friend and healer, and as you dedicate yourself to her, she dedicates herself to you.

IN A READING

Make peace and let go of past issues around being abandoned or not understood or of feeling unsupported, as those experiences need no longer colour your worldview. Trust that you belong here, and that your connection to the Earth Goddess will support you in all ways. You are sensitive, and rightly so. Never judge your sensitivity or feel that you are overreacting – but also allow nature to calm and soothe you, so that you can be focused on accomplishing your soul mission. If you feel that you are on your own, when you would like some help, allow the Divine Mother to be your friend and guide, whilst trusting that at the right moment, more allies will arrive. The Earth Mother has her own sense of timing, and you are not forgotten. You are just growing according to her wisdom and grace. Have faith in yourself and in her.

SPIRITUAL GUIDANCE

In the Māori worldview, humans are not seen as separate from, nor superior to, the natural world. Instead, humans are part of nature and have a sacred role to preserve and protect the Earth Mother, known as *Papatūānuku*. Her guardians are known as *Kaitiaki*, the ones who take action to defend her and safeguard her natural resources so that she – and we – can thrive.

There is an innate instinct in the human soul to seek an emotional connection with the natural world for pleasure and healing. When this connection is denied, which is the basis for all environmental abuse, the result is great suffering. The more soul you have, the more your personal identity becomes intertwined with nature and the greater the devastation you will feel in the face of environmental degradation. This is not being overly sensitive. This is being awake at a soul level.

Disconnection from the Divine Feminine harms humanity in ways that eventually lead us to psychological pain and physical disease. Perfectionism, impatience, thinking about what we can get, instead of what we can give, all these erode self-esteem and emotional fulfilment. They distort what is meant to be sacred sexuality into a performance, a perpetuation of emotional wounding and abuse, which drains our creative power and prevents us from being able to feel for our truths. Then we end up feeling confused, anxious and uncertain about our future. These are signs that we need to heal and strengthen our connection to the natural world, to restore our connection to the Sacred Feminine.

The Kaitiaki soul can help us reconnect to the Divine Feminine, rather than dismiss, exploit and use her. Loving our

Mother and feeling respect and reverence for her will restore our vitality and energy and help us gain a sense of wellbeing. You intuitively understand the need for this sort of relationship to the Earth, and you must remember to cultivate your connection so as to grow peace in your soul.

It is part of your destiny to read the wisdom of the ancient lineages from which you have evolved – from those ancestors who lived in a world very different to ours, who knew how to sustain themselves in harmony with the natural world over long periods of time, and who can help us remember that life requires a sustainable relationship with the Earth Mother. Their wisdom is encoded in the natural world. Through taking the time to tune into the Earth, you are one who can read her records and share the wisdom teachings that you perceive. Honour your ability to be a devotee of the Mother Earth. Allow her and your own courage and intelligence to empower you on your path, to support you in speaking your truths, especially when they go against the grain. For is that not what creation is all about, opening up to something new?

HEALING PROCESS

Re-earthing is a sacred practice to help you plug into the consciousness of the Earth Goddess in a truly grounded, healing and nurturing way. In this way, you both receive from her and become more able to give to her, through your increasing attainment of your life's work and personal wellbeing.

To re-earth yourself, spend a little time each day in physical contact with the earth. Physical touch – barefoot or with hands on dirt and grass or on the trunk of a tree – is sufficient for this process.

A beautiful addition to this healing process is to say a simple prayer or statement to the earth at the beginning and end of your re-earthing practice. It might be 'I love you,' at the start, and 'Thank you,' at the end. Or it could be a deeper and more personal conversation about gratitude, hope and trust and about the wise use of your creative power or your concerns about the world. You might ask for her assistance and guidance so that you can honour the Divine Feminine in the best way possible, according to your talents and abilities.

The more you do this practice, the more love and devotion will arise and the stronger and more conscious your connection with the Earth Mother will be, and the more empowered you shall become to fulfil your destiny. Don't be afraid to lean on her, to need her and to let her help you help yourself and the world.

11. AIYANA VISION

Way of the Divine Feminine Revealed

11. AIYANA VISION
Way of the Divine Feminine Revealed

The Divine Feminine yearns to reveal her way and her wisdom to you that you may live passionately and purposefully. As you trust her inner guiding voice, you recognise the authentic desires and visions that move you from within, that are the seeds of your sacred mission. You shall experience the clarity and soul-deep relief that only truth can bring. You shall experience a knowing of purpose that awakens your ability to live deliberately and experience deep fulfilment.

IN A READING

Aiyana Vision is the blossoming awareness of your life purpose and true inner passion. You are being lovingly pushed to admit to your authentic and most passionate soul yearnings, becoming bold with honesty. What means so much to you that you are willing to give up all that you have held on to out of fear so that it may be? What matters enough to you that you would symbolically die and be reborn – with all the endings and uncertainty such growth entails – so that your dream can become real? Don't turn away from your yearning out of fear, practicality or any other excuse to replace faith with doubt. Your truth acknowledged will bring you peace, even if admitting it also means facing the personal transformation required to bring that truth to life in your world. When it is truth, it is healing. Embrace it.

SPIRITUAL GUIDANCE

You are due for a revelation, an awakening into deeper recognition and understanding of your true spiritual passion and sacred life purpose – and all that is entailed in manifesting it in loving co-creation with the Universe.

The situations, behaviours and relationships that were appropriate and acceptable at earlier stages of your life journey will not necessarily continue to be so as your spiritual path progresses. Notice the effect of people, places and situations on your state of mind. Such effects could be uplifting and helpful. However, even if intentions are good, the effect may be diminishing, compromising your ability to hold connection to the light. You will know when that is happening because your inspiration, your idealism and your hope – all of which give you vital energy to work towards fulfilment of your most cherished dreams – slowly become tainted by lower frequency beliefs. Instead of trusting, you become fearful and impatient. Instead of being true to your original vision, you believe that you must change yourself to suit the world. Instead of feeling happiness and confidence in your ability to complete your tasks, you feel overwhelmed, inadequate and insecure.

From a place of wisdom rather than fearfulness, take care of what sort of energy you allow to have direct and unfettered access to your inner being. Such a position of potential influence over your state of mind is best reserved for the Divine Mother. You will know when a message or impression is coming from a pure place because of what happens in your being in response to it. You will feel happy, at peace, willing and capable, even in the face of challenge. You will have a sense that all things are working as they are meant to – and, although you will be more relaxed, you will also be more focused, productive and inspired. Genuine divine guidance does not create anxiety, nor does it paint something to be well when it is in need of repair. Yet no matter the content of the message, you will feel relief in the face of such loving and helpful truth. If someone or something has stolen away your peace of mind and certainty of heart, use the healing process below, and your own intention, to claim it back.

There is a vision unfolding within your being, an urging of the Sacred Feminine, something which deep within your bones you recognise as being truth. It may still be blossoming into fullness, but if you tune in to yourself, you can feel the essence of its beauty and grace. It is not wishful thinking or fantasy. Do not give up on your beautiful visions.

HEALING PROCESS
Place your attention on the image of the oracle card, seeing the peaceful love in the eyes of the goddess as she gazes gently into the depths of you. Her gaze can evoke certain feelings in you – of being deeply loved and nurtured, of being seen at an honest and deep level with absolute acceptance.

Whisper kind and loving words to yourself, as if the image were speaking to you. You may like to repeat the words below, several times over to yourself in a soothing voice. You can also create your own words of love if you wish.

I love you. I am here for you. All is well. I trust you unconditionally. My faith in you never waivers. I will always care for you. I am always by your side and in your heart. Together, we shall ensure your divine fulfilment for the greatest good of all life.

Then say this prayer aloud: *I invite the unconditional love of the Sacred Mother to heal my mind, body and soul. I open to your true guidance, to the vision of beauty that you hold for me this lifetime and all the resources that you give so generously that I may fulfil my being and my destiny. May your truth calm my mind and bring divine knowledge to my heart. I trust in the truth of what your perfect will holds in store for me. I need no fear. I embrace your loving presence within my heart.*

Assume a relaxing, comfortable position, perhaps taking a seated posture or lying down, wrapped up in a blanket or shawl or hugging yourself or nestling next to your pet – or even stretching out delightedly on your back, like a star fish.

Rest for as long as feels right for you.

You have completed your healing process.

12. AMUATA

Sage of Higher Knowledge

Seek what feels true, even beyond the logical. If something doesn't feel right, challenge it and dig deeper. Educate and inform yourself on matters of importance to you. Trust that your mind is strong and bright enough to do this. Enhance your self-esteem by researching for information and trusting your intuition to help you discern what is useful and true. Have faith in your own mental abilities. If others have criticised you or made you feel inadequate in understanding, cast that off as belonging to the past and not relevant to you now. You will become immune to manipulation by others, who may be convincing but not necessarily accurate or helpful. Trust the power of your mind to receive and recognise the answers that you need. You will find your way.

IN A READING

Test all opinions, advice, research and alleged facts according to your own intuition and instinct. Select that which is helpful for you and notice that which is best cast aside, even if just for a time. Seek information and assistance from those that you feel can assist you –and yet place no human advisor above the ultimate, divine authority, which will guide you on how to proceed through a deep inner knowing. There is always new knowledge beyond existing boundaries of thought. We simply need to be open and willing to receive it with patience, discernment and trust in the greater guiding power. The oracle of Amuata comes to you with guidance that an answer is coming, an important piece of information, and that when you are centred in your heart you will recognise that for what it is and know how to proceed.

SPIRITUAL GUIDANCE

Intuition and instinct are two forms of intelligence, one arising from the heart and the other from the wisdom of the body. These special forms of knowing are essential for living a wise and authentic life, one that is tuned into the love and truth that flows through our Universe. Intuition can help us know without knowing how we know, showing us an accurate birds-eye view of a situation in a sudden flash of insight. Instinct can give us a stark and honest gut feeling about the intentions of another person or the real value of an opportunity. You do not need to have a logical explanation to justify your intuitive and instinctive recognition of falsehood, deception or other misleading uses of information. These two forms of intelligence are ways of sacred feminine knowing.

Then there are logic and intellect, which can also be gifts for humanity to use for great effect. Provided that logic and intellect are not used to cut off from sacred feminine knowing, they can play a very helpful role in living a happy and fulfilling life. Finding the correct information in this age – when there is an abundance of information with varying degrees of truth and helpfulness – is an important skill to develop. We can do this with a combination of logic and intuition. Sometimes intuition and instinct will tell you that a piece of information accepted by others is not actually true for you. That sacred feminine intelligence recognises truth and is able to guide you as to how to best use it for your noble goals.

The oracle of Amuata comes to you with guidance suggesting that you take your time to inform yourself. If you have a decision to make, trust your instincts and your intuition above and beyond logic or other people's opinions, but make sure that you obtain the information that you feel is most useful to your decision-making process. Amuata urges you to take care around simply accepting the opinion or point of view of another, even if that person has been a trusted guide for a time or has many credentials. Sometimes your inner knowing shall encourage you to a different course of action, even if you have great respect for the person offering their opinion. The Universe may simply have other plans for you.

If you have ever been put down or judged as not being clever enough, or if your intellect has been worshipped and encouraged at the expense of the intuitions of your heart, the oracle of Amuata comes to you now with a message of healing relief. There are many ways of knowing, and we are all unique in our particular combinations of intellect, instinct, intuition and insight. You have been created exactly as you were meant to be for sacred purpose. The judgements of others – for better or worse – are meaningless. What matters is that you find your own best way of sensing truth, honouring when something does not feel right and moving forward when something rings true.

HEALING PROCESS

Find a place to relax. Say this prayer aloud: *I call upon the grace of unconditional love and the truth of the divine mind to empty and cleanse my mind and emotional body from fixed opinion, half-truths and deceptions. May I trust and be patient so that I can see and know the highest level of truth available to me. May I give and receive peace, enlightenment and helpful, accurate communication. May divine light shine bright and help all beings find their way. Through my own free will, so be it.*

Relax now for as long as you need. Perhaps close your eyes and focus on your breathing for several moments, as you allow the power of your prayer to work at a spiritual level and beyond. Allow yourself to become empty and still and go into as deep a relaxation as possible, for as long as feels good for you.

You have completed your healing process.

13. IXCHEL

Medicine of the Rainbow Jaguar

13. IXCHEL
Medicine of the Rainbow Jaguar

Ixchel protects you now, as you transition from one life phase to the next. With her rainbow light, this guardian goddess instructs you on how to use great power with wisdom, to nourish only what is worthy. Using Jaguar medicine, with perfect timing, she confronts that which is unworthy of her devotion, eradicating destructive forces and creating space for healing relief and rebirth. Her presence is the wild power of the jaguar, the renewal promise of the rainbow and divine feminine creativity. All darkness shall be overcome.

IN A READING

You are going through a transition. Cultivate hope and stay true to your intentions. Let nothing divert you from your true path. If you have a new project, vision or lifestyle that you are seeking to bring into the world, Ixchel is guiding and guarding you for a healthy birth. She also brings a message that there are times when fierceness is necessary. It is important that you cut off negative sources completely at this time and do not allow yourself to be used or exploited. This is not the time to indulge someone else's ego or go against your own inner knowing in order to give someone the benefit of the doubt. Trust your instincts and break immediately from what isn't right for you. This will bring you new opportunities and situations that are worthy of your passionate devotion.

SPIRITUAL GUIDANCE

Ixchel, goddess of the rainbow light, is responsible for sending rain to nourish the crops, ensuring fertility and life. She overturns her divine womb and allows sacred, life-giving rain to fall into the soul, promoting growth. The rainbow light of Ixchel is an oracle of renewal. This is your sign that all is in accord with life, that new beginnings shall stem from the past, that there is power to create and that what is beautiful, necessary and healing shall flow to you, and through you, into the world.

Ixchel holds Jaguar medicine. Jaguar thrives in many environments, being able to climb, run, and swim. Because of its mastery over height, distance and water, it is said at a spiritual level to hold power throughout all dimensions. Its medicine brings the ability to move in darkness without fear, to see clearly through chaos, to evade and to destroy. Jaguar medicine is fierce, decisive, powerful and irreversible. Ixchel brings you this medicine now for your own soul journey. A definitive conquering of darkness is at hand.

Ixchel's teachings include her story of falling passionately in love with a man who did not respect her. Eventually, to get away from him, she shapeshifted into a jaguar, becoming invisible whenever he sought her out. In this way, she evaded him and saved herself – and the world which relied upon her bounty and vitality – from destruction. Ixchel teaches us of the need to confront what isn't working in our lives, including the influence of negative people, honestly, without fear or compromise. Jaguar is not a half-way medicine. If we allow unworthy influences to take up residence in our minds, our hearts, our souls – even just a little – they will eventually be our undoing, eroding our happiness, self-esteem, vitality and ability to fulfil our passionate purpose. Ixchel brings Jaguar to remind us that exploitation, abuse and disrespect are unacceptable and must be dealt with effectively, according to correct timing and with absolute certainty in our hearts. This is not about harming another but about cutting off their influence in our souls.

Jaguar medicine is a great power and can be used for good or ill. Purity of heart and mind becomes increasingly important as spiritual power grows. Make yourself unavailable to negativity, gossip or ill will in any way. Seek out the honest and the constructive. Share your power and devotion judiciously, and only with that which serves your true values.

HEALING PROCESS

Find a place to relax. Feel or imagine that there is a rainbow starting at your left side, arcing over your head and landing on your right side. The right side then arcs underneath you and joins back up with the start of the rainbow on your left. You now have an oval rainbow shape around you.

Say aloud: *The rainbow light brings me healing, blessing and spiritual grace now, according to unconditional divine love. The Divine Mother brings me all that I need with such generosity and wisdom.*

Rest in this rainbow light, allowing it to bring you healing. All you need to do is relax for as long as feels right.

When you are ready, say aloud: *Jaguar medicine honours my soul and divine love now.*

Allow yourself to feel, imagine or visualise that there is a jaguar emerging from the depths of your soul. The muscular, lean body pulsates with power, even in rest. This potency bristles just beneath your skin, and a layer of fur rests above your skin. Your head is sturdy and broad. Your jaw, which you can open wide, is powerful, and your tongue is loose and long. You use your senses to see without seeing. You are aware of the space all around you, in all directions, missing nothing.

Let yourself feel more vital and alive now. Your teeth are fangs. Your fingernails and toenails, are sharp claws extending. On your next exhalation, bare your fangs. Do not direct this energy towards a person, but rather towards an energy of negativity. Use your claws to swipe through what is no longer needed. Jaguar doesn't need a lot of movement to be effective – one shearing swipe is enough.

The medicine has provided its remedy. Rest as your jaguar form fades. Your human soul emerges cleansed and renewed. Bring your attention back to the rainbow light that surrounds you. Allow it to concentrate itself gently into the depths of your soul. Rest for as long as you need.

You have completed your healing process.

14. CLAN OF THE WOLF HEART

We Are the Ones We've Been Waiting For

You belong to the Clan of the Wolf Heart. This is a soul tribe, with boundaries beyond bloodlines and geography. It is based on soul connection to love's wisdom and higher truths of Great Spirit. The Clan is united through Wolf medicine and the heart. These are the qualities of the Divine Feminine that unify, allowing for a palpable experience of oneness that brings power to our collective wisdom and purpose.

IN A READING

Reach out for help from others, whilst you honour and respect your individuality and your own unique life journey. Balance social time with taking care of your own individual needs, including the need for time out in solitude to hear your inner truths and renew yourself. Anger can be a sign from the soul, a sacred gift that asks you to deal with a situation, to bring about something different and more empowering. Use your anger as a sacred gift with compassion and clear purpose. Fight wholeheartedly when you need to safeguard what truly matters. Be open to a greater guiding wisdom so that you know when to be merciful and when to cut something off completely. Believe in the power of your inner voice, and do not silence yourself.

SPIRITUAL GUIDANCE

Through the Wolf Heart, we are soul kin. Whilst our external identities may shift and change with circumstance, our soul tribe is fixed in the heart of the wolf way. It is the backbone of the emerging new world culture. This began as alternative culture, but it is now growing stronger in numbers, becoming more pervasive in consciousness, in influence, in power. It is rising up as the saving grace, guiding the human race into new order. Because our personalities are strong and we are not afraid to voice our individual truths, we may get our buttons pushed by each other at times. However, when we remember that we are on the same team, fighting for the same greater purpose, we can forgive and encourage each other, not take it too personally and continue to effectively harness the power of what we can accomplish together.

Wolf medicine bestows the qualities of endurance, inner wisdom and community. Wolves mate for life and the wolf clan has an organised social structure that includes a balance between group endeavour and individualism. The social order of the wolves provides support, loyalty and thriving – and yet wolves are free-spirited animals. Wolf wisdom teaches us how to balance solitude and socialisation. It teaches that both are needed for the wellbeing of ourselves and our clan. Wolf wisdom teaches us to share ourselves without losing ourselves.

The howl of the wolf is primal and powerful. It is used to locate clan members or to define the boundaries of their territory to wolves from outside of the pack. The howling wolf is medicine for standing your ground and defending that which is rightfully within your guardianship. If this strikes a note within you now, be aware that using your voice and your energy to set boundaries and claim your space is important. The territory is not physical. That is the way of the ego. The territory is spiritual. Claiming it means reclaiming and sustaining the right state of mind and the expanded consciousness of openheartedness to the Divine that allows you to determine the quality, consciousness and stability of that space for all beings that seek refuge within it.

Wolf medicine is the awakening of the pathfinder, the way-shower, the teacher. Wolf can learn new ways and teach them to others. Part of your soul purpose is to guide and inspire others through what you learn to master in your own life. We are the people who can do what's needed. We can fight the status quo, ravage the human mind away from inadequate responsiveness – and elicit soul passion and on-the-ground action to take us from merely salvaging what we can into alchemical eco-salvation and the birthing of a new world order.

Let us recognise ourselves as the empowered ones. The Divine has blessed the Tribe of the Wolf Heart with intelligence, individuality, social and community values, commitment and ability to outwit enemies, protect and defend what matters and adapt to change successfully. May we realise our abilities, tap into the resources we have and use them fruitfully. May we have joyful courage and confidence in who we are and what we are here to do.

HEALING PROCESS

Say aloud: *My spirit claims divine territory upon the earth. I trust in the supernatural ability of my soul to determine, shift and enforce the spiritual territory under my rightful guardianship as a way-shower and pathfinder. I accept all divine blessing to fulfil the soul purpose of the Wolf Way, providing protection and sanctuary for those beings within my care. I give to and receive from my soul tribe with a willing heart empowered in the Wolf Way. May we be blessed and guided by Great Spirit to fulfil our destinies, and inspire each other, as the ways of darkness are overcome by ways of light.*

Close your eyes and relax.

Visualise, feel or pretend that you can feel your heart from the inside, a beautiful open space. Within that heart is a gleaming wild wolf. Feel its heightened senses. Notice the colour of its fur, its eyes and the power and vitality that radiates from this spiritual guide. Does it have a message for you?

You may see, sense or feel other wolves in your heart or around you. Allow the wolf in the centre of your heart to be empowered, safe and supported, even if there are challengers. Feel the strength and divinity of that central inner wolf, as it is connected to a sustaining and unyielding divine power of truth, peace and wisdom.

Be with this for as long as feels right for you.

You have finished your healing process.

15. AJNA DURGA

Power of the Good

15. AJNA DURGA
Power of the Good

You need never lose faith in the power of good. You need never lose faith in how much you can accomplish as an independent and inspired individual in this world. You need never believe that you are alone or without divine protection. You need never fear evil. The third eye of the Divine Mother sees all things, is ever watchful and ever just. She births, through holy vision, the manifest power of good in all realms. Her gaze is upon you now. Trust her.

IN A READING

Believe in the power of the Divine to keep an eye on things for you. Trust that power to alert you when you need to know something or to understand what is happening in your life and what you need – even if you aren't so sure of that yourself at times. Be active in contesting negativity. The moment you feel something isn't coming from love, acknowledge it immediately. You don't have to make it about you or analyse it. Use your divine connection to deal with it promptly and effectively. Call for divine support in all things. You will not divert help away from someone else if you ask for it for yourself. When you allow yourself to be helped, this empowers your path, which, in turn, helps all beings. Divine assistance is always there for you unconditionally. If you are not thinking the best thoughts, divine support will correct your thoughts. Never hesitate to call for that support. It is your greatest ally. Give up your attachment to past experiences of rejection and abandonment so that you can open up to how much the Divine loves you and can help you. Practice feeling the confidence and unconditional trust in a higher power, knowing it is stronger than all else.

SPIRITUAL GUIDANCE

In the Hindu pantheon of divine beings, Durga shines bright as a powerful warrior goddess and protector of the good and true. She is the unified potency of all divine forces of goodness against negativity and evil. An icon for independence and divine power of the light, Durga is the solar mother who shines light, restores order and protects the human soul by destroying impurities such as jealousy, hatred, anger and selfishness. She is creative, inventive, responsive and powerful. Once, a particularly adept demon looked like he was getting the upper hand in battle with her, so Durga promptly birthed Kali out of her third eye. Kali, the black goddess, ferociously destroyed the demon immediately. Durga is the Invincible One. The Sanskrit word *durga* means fort, a place that is protected in battle and unable to be overcome. Durga's power animal is the tiger, indicating her unlimited power to protect virtue and destroy evil. She is bright. She is swift. She is unconquerable goodness.

When Durga comes into view, you have been fighting against negative energies at some level of your being – whether obviously in the world or more deeply within your own soul. If you do not acknowledge this, you may fall prey to unnecessary confusion and self-doubt, believing that the issue is solely a psychological matter to deal with. Rather, it is a spiritual issue requiring divine intervention and protection, which is now offered to you. It is helpful to remember that evil is not about people, but about the forces that operate through them with ill intent. Durga is an inextinguishable light, and she is rising within you now. Her presence reminds you of the light that is divine and true and therefore cannot ever be subject to any lesser power such as hate, fear, jealousy, spite or greed. No matter how intimidating an opponent or situation may seem, they are no match for the sacred rage of the divine goddess of light and justice, who vanquishes the evil that haunts their souls and perpetuates distress.

Durga is your ally, your divine weapon, your refuge and your vital energy for sacred purpose. Do not allow yourself to be intimidated. You can be confident within yourself and go about your work. You need not explain yourself or justify your actions to anyone other than the Divine and your own heart. Do not turn away from any obstacle. Believe in the power of the Divine to clear the path for you, and the path shall be cleared. Believe that you are held in the fort of divine light. Let that confidence and trust in the divine goddess of goodness radiate out of you like a shining sun that fills your heart, your mind and your belly. If your confidence has diminished because of past attacks or encounters with those who are so toxic that they cannot – or will not – recognise the difference between constructive communication and verbal, emotional, psychic or physical abuse, then take heart. You are blessed with divine intervention, protection and healing. Your confidence and sense of personal and spiritual power shall be fully restored and will actually increase through this experience of healing. You shall discover the peace and confidence that comes from the realisation that love can never be conquered.

HEALING PROCESS

Say aloud: *Unconditionally loving light of Durga, bless my endeavours and relationships with your divine light and protection. Hold me in the fort of divine goodness, where I am unharmed. Your beauty and truth shine light into any darkness, keeping me safe and blessed in grace. May your divine justice prevail. So be it.*

Say or sing this chant for as many times as feels good: *Om Dum Durgayei Namaha* (Sounds like, *om doom door-guy-yay nam-ah-haah*.)

Place your hands firmly on your belly and then on your heart. Pause for a moment. Then bow your head with your hands in prayer.

You have completed your healing process.

16. LOLO

Stand in the Light

You are unique. You are a divine and beautiful being. You stand apart from the crowd. Sometimes this evokes jealousy or desire in others who want to possess your light and beauty as their own. You need never fear another or believe that they can harm you. Allow yourself to be true to who you are. Do not try to hide your inner light and beauty. You are meant to be seen. Your soul is nurtured and protected by your love for Great Spirit.

IN A READING

Don't avoid the spotlight or try to hide yourself nor dull your light to appease another or your own fears. Your true inner divine light and beauty is meant to help others, and the only way that can occur is if you allow yourself to fully be and express it. Do not shrink away from your magnificence when you feel challenged. Instead step it up to an entirely new level of boldness! You have a gentle nature, but you are strong. If you have become obsessed with the beauty or power of another, it's time to come back to your own divine beauty, to unearth it, explore it, express it and let it shine. Trying to blend in will drain the energy from you. Let those who are attracted to your light adapt to your level of divine expression. You are the benchmark, and they will evolve to reach you.

SPIRITUAL GUIDANCE

In Malagasy, the language of Madagascar, *lolo* means 'butterfly', 'moth' and 'soul'. The sunset moth of Madagascar is big, beautiful and bright. Whilst most moths are nocturnal, creatures that are active at night, the sunset moth of Madagascar is a creature of the day. With iridescent wings creating a kaleidoscopic effect as they refract the light, they are considered by some to be the most beautiful insect on earth. Yet, in subdued light, their wings can appear far less remarkable. Without light, their true beauty cannot be recognised. You, like this unique creature, are a being that needs light – light to nourish your life force, and light to reveal your true and remarkable divine beauty. You are meant to shine your divinity in the world in the daylight, not keep it hidden under the cloak of night, for fear of how others may react.

The bright colours and shape of the sunset moth's wings, and their presence in the full light of day, leads many to mistake these unique moths for butterflies. You, too, will find that people do not always realise who and what you are. They may mistakenly assume that your joy and beauty indicate that life has always been easy for you. They may fail to recognise the true depth of your soul and the experiences of darkness and struggle that you have overcome to become the vibrant, beautiful being that you can now be seen to be.

During the daylight hours, the sunset moth can be seen flitting from one flower to another, feeding on nectar. They discern light waves and indicate a strong preference for white flowers, although not for specific plants. You are one of the rare souls who can find the truth of light and love in any number of spiritual or religious paths, in any number of situations. You are able to recognise and be nourished by purity in many forms – be it a random act of kindness from a stranger, the unconditional love of an animal, a genuine blessing from a spiritual master or a moment of simple beauty in nature. You can sense the true presence of love through an evolved, inner spiritual discernment.

The Madagascar sunset moths are very particular in their eating habits. They are attracted to the nectar of plants that other creatures tend to avoid, because they cannot metabolise the toxins. For the sunset moth, however, what they are drawn to consume is not harmful to them. Instead, these moths become poisonous to predators by simply following their natural instincts to nurture themselves according to what suits them – even though it would not necessarily suit any other creature in the same way. What nurtures and nourishes you, what feels good for you heart, body and soul, is also what protects you. You actually don't need to do anything else for effective protection than place yourself in the divine beauty of what you love absolutely and completely.

HEALING PROCESS

If you are concerned about negative attitudes or attacking behaviours from others for any reason, you can use this healing process to clear the fear and reinforce your divine sanctuary.

Close your eyes and relax.

Focus on the flow of your breath in and out. Imagine that you can drape yourself in a cloak of divine beauty, light and glory. This cloak is as light as a feather, shining with endless iridescent shades of colour that reveal the exquisite beauty of the Divine.

This cloak flows lightly around you, offering you a sense of having wings, or having a body that is beyond your physical body, and yet interpenetrates it, too. That body of light and colour can breathe, as though it is lightly aerated all over. It can release anything that is not of love and shines forth a continuous stream of beautiful, divine light in all directions. This light body can move freely, growing as large as you wish, taking any shape, any size and any form that feels beautiful to your heart. Allow whatever your experience is to be.

When you are ready, say aloud: *I am cloaked in divine glory, light, grace and beauty. I am a child of the Divine and am protected in the sanctuary of absolute divine love, now and always. So be it.*

Dance, meditate, rest or pray with your cloak around you now, if you wish, and keep it with you for as long as you choose.

You have completed your healing process.

17. PADMA SUNDARI
Out of Darkness, the Light is Born

17. PADMA SUNDARI
Out of Darkness, the Light is Born

The light is powerful enough to survive exposure to the darker side of humanity and remain pure, empowered and effective. Trust in your spiritual purpose as a light in this world. Trust particularly in your ability to bring purity, order, grace and light to disorder, chaos and destruction. The Divine is ever by your side and ever within your heart, assisting you with this higher purpose in all ways.

IN A READING

All issues can be healed through the unlimited recourse and creative resourcefulness of the Divine. You are destined to be part of a creative solution for any issue that you have in your life or that exists in the world and touches your heart. The issue only exists so that divine genius can resolve it! Struggles are sometimes the best way for us to learn something we need to understand for our life journey. Trust that when you ask for help, even apparently impossible situations can be turned around. With willing human engagement and divine grace, there is more than enough light, healing, creative innovation, wisdom and energy available to keep Mother Earth and all her creatures, including humanity, thriving. Never give up your hope and trust in what is possible – nor your willingness to act upon that hope and trust.

SPIRITUAL GUIDANCE

The Divine Mother, in the form of Padma Sundari, is Lakshmi, the goddess of wealth, beauty, love and spiritual enlightenment, represented as a shining lotus. An ancient symbol for spiritual enlightenment, the lotus rests pure upon the muddy waters from which it has grown. Lakshmi's divine lotus flowers remind us that the spiritual light needs material form through which it can manifest itself in the world, as if it were divine electricity needing the lamp of the soul through which to give the gift of illumination. Without the lamp, the electricity cannot manifest its power, and without electricity, the lamp cannot fulfil its true purpose.

When the oracle of Padma Sundari appears, her message is that you are able to do a lot of good in this world. The Divine Mother will assist you with your purpose so that you succeed, but you must take action. Allow the light of spirit into your soul so that you never again feel that you are doing anything on your own. Remind yourself regularly you have a divine sponsor, guide, coach, partner and friend with you always. That friend has unlimited resources and the most powerful will of all. Notice how your confidence to take action increases when you build that belief system within you – how much more secure, courageous and willing you become.

Part of your spiritual path requires that you walk your talk and live in a way that shows optimism and practicality. When something's not working, we don't need to hide from it in shame. We face it because we have spiritual self-esteem and self-confidence. When we choose courage, we can confront what isn't working and are able to search for answers. Rather than becoming overwhelmed or afraid of any darkness, remember that the Holy Mother is with you and within you. With your active participation, she will bring you everything that you need to confront and tackle any issue, no matter how intimidating it may seem, one step at a time.

Along with the power of your divine connection, you have the intelligence and ability to find information, to educate yourself, to try out new behaviours so as to become an active part of the solution for any matter that moves you deeply. Taking these steps will boost your self-esteem and your energy levels, helping you to feel good about yourself and your presence in the world. It's not about being perfect, it's just about taking that next step for you. Trust in divine timing, realising that there is far-reaching good that can happen through you as you continue to be actively engaged with life and your inner divine relationship. Believe in what we can and will accomplish together, through our passionate love affair with Great Spirit and our adoring devotion to the Earth Mother and her children.

HEALING PROCESS

If possible and practical, this exercise can be done barefoot. If you cannot physically move through the process, then visualise or imagine it, instead.

Stand comfortably, with knees slightly bent and feet about hip width apart. Allow your posture to be straight but relaxed.

Direct your awareness into your feet. You can help this process along by wiggling your toes a little, shifting your body weight slightly from heels to toes and side to side, and rising up onto your toes and back on your heels if your balance is good today. Imagine that you can feel your feet from the inside.

Imagine, feel or intend that your feet can sense the energy of the earth, rich, nourishing and vitalising, in the ground beneath you. Imagine and intend that the magnetic pulling power of your feet is strong enough to create a palpable connection – a gentle suctioning motion – between your feet and the energy of the earth. Allow the earth energy to build up beneath your feet and then flow up through your being, softly out through the top of your head, gently cascading down on either side of you, soaking back into the ground.

Say aloud: *I call upon divine grace and unconditional love to show me truth and creative solutions, empowered by divine wisdom, for all matters in my life, including (mention anything particular or specific here that you would like help to resolve or heal). May all beings know and be blessed, assisted and empowered by the Divine Mother to fulfil their purpose and potential. So be it.*

Place your hands in prayer.

You have finished your healing process.

18. KUNTUR YACHAK

Blessings from the Sun of Hana Pacha

Condor swiftly brings the will of Great Spirit to earth, through the gift of powerful medicine. Despite great odds, even in the face of what may appear to be an inevitable defeat, extraordinary triumph is at hand. This is the prophecy of resurrection, of the rising up of what was thought to be lost. It shall happen with unexpected and surprising swiftness. Your divine destiny is now held in the guiding hand of a great spiritual master.

IN A READING

Condors are born with their eyes open, but do not have vocal chords to speak. You have always seen clearly – trust in this, even if you struggle to find the words to express all that you see. Condors reveal emotion through changes in their skin colour. This is a reminder to trust what your body is telling you. Your bodily intuition is a form of wisdom. You have a spiritual connection to the cosmic Christ Consciousness, the universal Sacred Heart seeking to awaken itself in humanity. Your divine life purpose involves assuming the role of leader, guide, healer and Earth Warrior for love on this planet, in your own unique way. An inviolable spiritual protection surrounds you.

SPIRITUAL GUIDANCE

Kuntur, or 'condor', is the ancient bird of the Andes. Once flying alongside sabre-toothed tigers, this, the largest flying bird in the world, is also one of the oldest species on earth. Soaring to great heights, and for hours at a time, with little or no movement of its wings, condor holds the medicine of strength, spiritual connection and grace. With a lifespan similar to that of a human being and the ability to soar at exceptional speed, it also carries the gifts of longevity and swiftness. Condor has been on the brink of extinction many times, yet it still survives, even in the wild. At the top of the food chain, the condor is rarely a hunter, taking life. Feeding off carrion instead, its medicine brings cleansing and protection as it is able to process toxins that would be harmful to other creatures.

The predator of the condor, and also the guardian that has enabled it to crawl back from near-extinction into wildness again, is humanity. Through collective wisdom and co-operation between various disciplines and industries, human beings have been able to restore with wisdom what was nearly destroyed in ignorance. Condor is an affirmation of the power we have to undo damage and create extraordinary healing – but we have to listen, we have to actively respond, and we have to work together in conscious collaboration.

Condor is the medicine of the shaman or *yachack*, the Andean healer, or 'one who knows'. In the Andean shamanic worldview, Condor rules the superior spiritual world, the first plane of pure spiritual beings, known as Hana Pacha. The sun of Hana Pacha is the shamanic Christ. In human form, this being is known as Yeshua or Jesus. In the language of spirit medicine, it is Condor.

The oracle of Kuntur Yachak brings a message straight from the universal Christ Consciousness, beating as the living sacred heart of Great Spirit. It is an offer of absolute protection that is strong enough to sustain your purity, integrity and effectiveness as you navigate the challenges inherent in the earthly world of Puma, known as Kay Pacha, and much needed protection over the unconscious world of Snake, known as Uhku Pacha. This protection ensures that your passionate purpose is not distorted or derailed by unconscious forces. As you accept this blessing, you shall know only protection, empowerment and grace as you manifest the spirit medicine of Condor, helping to bring hope, conscious and creative collaboration, dynamic sacred activism and miraculous restoration to the earth through her evolving human family.

HEALING PROCESS

Sit comfortably, with one hand on your heart.

Say aloud: *Through unconditional love and in service to the universal Sacred Heart, I invoke the prophecy of the eagle and the condor, that the opposites shall fly together in harmony once more and divine presence shall fill the earth and bless all of her children. The destiny of this world is to be love's paradise.*

Visualise, feel, intend or imagine that there is a beautiful being of light shining in your heart. This is Yeshua, the brother of love and divine essence fully manifested as a human being. He knows and loves you. He has complete spiritual mastery across the three worlds of Condor, Puma and Snake. At his right side, the eagle soars, and at his left side, the condor soars. They are in harmony, dancing in the skies. Beneath Yeshua's right foot is the puma, and beneath his left foot is the snake, in perfect peace, order and harmony. There is a profound sense of love and perfect cosmic order settling into all realms of existence, and into all aspects of your own being. This spiritual master brings with him the invisible presence of Great Spirit to restore and realign all of existence from the inside out. The truth and healing of this inner realignment brings a feeling of profound inner relief.

When you are ready, place a hand on your heart and say the following aloud: *Yeshua, Condor, Christ, loving friend of my soul, you cover me with your feathers. Under your wings I find refuge. Your divine perfection casts off fear and doubt, and through the invisible inner workings of Great Spirit, all is brought into correct order, now. May all beings thrive within the grace of Great Spirit. May all divine destinies be fulfilled. Through my own free will, so be it.*

Relax.

You have completed your healing process.

19. CHAKANA

Time to Cross the Threshold

A threshold appears, bringing an ending so complete that it is no longer possible to return to what has been. The light of the stars is your faithful guide into this new world. As you trust in your divine connection, deconstructed forms shall reshape themselves into relevant, helpful and beautiful new ways of living, thriving and expressing your true self. Trust in your strangest ideas, in that which is different, inspired or unconventional. This crossing is healing and furthers the activation of your divine potential.

IN A READING

Change is afoot. You won't feel in control of the process. Trust in what is new, different or exciting to you. Don't assume that unless all things happen easily, then you must be on the wrong path. You are on the correct path, even if the birthing pains to fulfil it are challenging. You are guided to reject societal norms about how you are supposed to live or what sort of things you are supposed to value. Instead, trust your own values and believe in the truths that you feel within your own heart. In time the world will be ready to recognise and benefit from your spiritual growth. The Universe is helping you in all ways, including through correct timing. At the right moment, you will leave the past behind you and enter into the fullness of the present moment, opening up to the brightness of your future.

SPIRITUAL GUIDANCE

The oracle of Chakana comes as a portent of crossing, a spiritual bridge between one world and another. The purpose of this is to increase spiritual light within you, promoting evolutionary revolution, a kind of healing alchemy, which cannot be undone. Chakana is an oracle of destiny, of events unfolding according to the greater movements of the heavens. This is a sign of a blessing, but it also requires conscious human participation so that the loving will of the heavens can manifest fully in the world for the benefit of all. Through how you choose to live, think and act, this sacred shift can benefit many lives, including your own. This oracle is a sign that destiny will meet with your personal efforts, and the result of this sacred convergence shall be the fulfilment of an inner potential, brought to life in the world.

Systems and belief structures based on disempowerment and inequality will ultimately fail. Perhaps not by one grand strike of love's army, but rather through the continual expression of new ideas that challenge the status quo, call attention to truth and invite an inspired vision of a new way that honours all from a place of spiritual equality. This is love in action, chipping away at that which would otherwise enslave the human soul in fear. It starts within us. It is the movement of consciousness destabilising the old ways of domination and darkness, paving the way for the emergence of a new consciousness of wisdom, discernment and love.

When your journey requires that you stand apart from the crowd, don't be afraid to embrace your outsider status and the freedom it bestows upon you – to think differently and objectively analyse what isn't working with the clarity that comes with a more remote point of observation. Your unconventional views may cause discomfort to some at first, but it is of the good sort. This sort of discomfort can stimulate a healing crisis, a divine disruption that cracks faulty belief systems, making way for inspired innovation and radical improvement. It is through the failure of that which cannot take us where we need to go that the new ideas which can are able to come to the fore. Things not working out as we had anticipated is nothing to fear. It is often mistaken as a 'no' from the Universe, but it is really just saying, 'There's a better way.'

There will be those that lead humanity into the new world, and those that try to hold on to the old ways. You are part of the spiritual spearhead piercing through established and unhealthy paradigms. Do not be disheartened by absence of support at first – nor by risk, or the possibility that the birthing of your idea into the world may take a longer time than you wished. Do not be concerned if most do not yet understand where you are coming from, or if resources are scarce at this time, as other more recognised or conventional points of view are granted more support in the world. Have faith, because once the time has come for the alternative view to take root and grow, the success shall be swift and far reaching. Persevere and keep your faith in the right outworks of all matters according to a higher plan. Time is working in your favour, so don't resist it. This oracle comes with divine promise: Your time shall come.

HEALING PROCESS

Stand comfortably with your arms above your head, reaching for the heavens.

Gently guide your arms down until your hands rest lightly on your heart.

Then continue to lower your arms, outstretching them again as they reach towards the earth.

Say aloud: *May the unconditional love of Hana Pacha, of the celestial grace of the Divine, bless the highest expression of pure love on this planet through all systems, all beings, all creations. May my destiny, and the loving destiny of all Earth Warriors, manifest through unconditional love and divine grace for the greatest good. May Kay Pacha, the lives of all in the here and now, know the grace of divine love made manifest. May Uqha Pacha, the deeper realms of existence, provide energy filtered through the purifying veil of unconditional love so as to serve the greatest good of all. So be it.*

Repeat the three steps with your arms again, finishing in prayer position at your heart.

You have completed your healing process.

20. CH'ASKA

Star of Venus

Ch'aska, Star of Venus, supports an inner shift to higher consciousness. Whether or not you consider yourself to be financially skilful, part of your sacred power and purpose includes the healing of economic and financial matters in your own life and the world. You are meant to experience abundance, creating and sharing prosperity from a place of inner spiritual security. A healing liberation from poverty consciousness allows the Universe to work through you more easily, without the obstruction of negative conditioning.

IN A READING

Financial healing is indicated. Let go of fear and trust unconditionally that the Universe is supporting you. What brings you a sense of joy, purpose and passionate devotion? Focus on that. Believe in your ability to thrive by being and expressing your authentic self. Notice how you relax into flow and more easily attract what you need when you acknowledge that the Universe wants you to flourish through being you. Focus on putting your beautiful beliefs out into the world, not in consuming the negativity or fear of others. Give of your spirit abundantly! Nothing is beyond the reach of divine assistance. Trust in this, and you can fulfil your purpose of being a positive influence in the world.

SPIRITUAL GUIDANCE

The oracle of Ch'aska is the oracle of Venus, the morning and evening star. She heralds the transition into a new reality of higher consciousness and healed experience regarding money, financial power and resources. This oracle guides you to give up false shame of not having enough, or guilt for having too much. Your true worth is a matter of soul and has nothing to do with material things. As you relax and acknowledge the love that the Universe has for you, your material reality will unfold with grace and divine support.

Place your sense of security not in the amount of money you have, but in the unconditional love and endless generosity that the Universe wishes to share with you. Trust that the Universe will provide you with all you need to fully live your life. When you are given something, accept it and consult your own heart for how you might share that resource with wisdom. Give yourself permission to stop making financial matters an issue in your own mind. Trust that the Universe knows what it's doing and all matters can be resolved according to a loving higher intelligence.

Focus on giving of your gifts to the world as generously as you can, whilst opening up to receive fully and fearlessly. As a sacred change-maker, you are asked to broaden your definition of currency from pertaining only to money to include that which has meaning for you at a soul level. This may include integrity, authenticity, relationship, consciousness and community. In your relationship with yourself and others, how might you express such a currency of soul? Seek and treasure that which cannot be quantified monetarily. Cultivate and share your experience of true wealth in the best and broadest sense. Some indigenous cultures define this wealth not as how much you accumulate for personal gain, but by how much you are able to give in support of your community.

This creation and honouring of soul currency does not mean that you are to be denied money or financial healing – it is about placing that in correct context. It shifts fear of lack into trust in Spirit. The recognition of soul currency helps unravel an obsession with money, freeing your mind and emotions to be reordered into a more relaxed and open attitude towards financial matters. This, in turn, makes it easier for you to receive the generous flow of abundance from the Universe. Seeing wealth as more than money, and refusing to make money an indication of success and the worth of a person, is the antidote to the wound of separateness. That wound creates selfishness, ignorance, jealousy and greed, stealing from community and depriving future generations their rightful inheritance.

This is the conscious economics of bringing people together, not driving them apart. When it is wisely placed within a soulful hierarchy and definition of value, not above it or beyond it, money can be part of a more full and sacred relationship of exchange – not something that creates division. We feel happier, more connected and at peace. A spirit of hope, optimism, inspiration and boldness of belief takes hold of our hearts, and we begin to feed the malnourished souls on this planet with good spiritual food. We no longer wait for the new world – we become it.

HEALING PROCESS
Place one hand on your heart and say aloud: *I give thanks for the abundance of grace available for all beings. I open my heart to let*

go of diminishing beliefs and interpretations of events. I no longer carry fear in my heart. My heart is filled with trust and peace. I give thanks for divine intervention, innovation and blessing on behalf of all beings, in all matters of economics. Great Spirit of Love, please guide, assist and protect each one of us in all worldly matters.

Stand facing the west (or to your left, if you prefer). Hold out your left arm, palm facing upward, and say aloud: *By the evening star, I now give over to the great beloved Spirit all matters of concern, that they be held in your hand, resolved by your grace.*

Your hand may feel heavy at first, but hold it softly there until it feels light.

Stand facing the east (or to your right, if you prefer). Hold out your right arm, palm facing upward and say aloud: *By the morning star, the great, divine beloved Spirit now gifts me with all that I need for divine fulfilment, for the overflowing of divine grace into this world so that love will flourish through all beings.*

Feel your right hand as touched by the spiritual light of the morning star and blessed.

Place your hands in prayer.

You have completed your healing process.

21. DADIRRI

Hearing Truth

21. DADIRRI
Hearing Truth

There is a deeper truth that shall bring peace to your heart, offering you guidance, comfort and renewal. You are guided to turn within for your answers. Do not allow another to interrupt, influence or distort your personal, trusting relationship with the Divine. Allow Great Spirit to be your highest counsel always, and you shall never be led astray. You shall know the words to speak and the consciousness to hold to evoke healing and set things right. Listen, for deep within, truth is known.

IN A READING

Focus on what you know to be true by tuning into what you feel, and not focusing on appearances or the opinions of others. There is a voice of spirit deep within you. Any time you want or need guidance, you have the ability to tune in to that inner voice bringing peace, comfort and clarity. It takes courage to turn within, rather than putting your faith in the people and things of this world, but you have enough inner strength and wisdom to do this. The truth within has been spoken. Trust that you can hear it.

SPIRITUAL GUIDANCE

You have an intuitive ability to recognise truths of the spirit. *Dadirri* is an Australian Aboriginal term for the deep, spiritual practice of reflective and respectful listening. It is a deep listening for truth beyond physical words and their logical meaning. It is the way the shaman hears, with the soul.

Through the power of his or her own inner experiences, the shaman is able to create spiritual wisdom for the community, bringing balance and unity between the realm of Great Spirit and our Earth. As one who holds the potential power of the shaman, it is part of your soul journey to seek out deeper meaning, to never assume that the whole truth is revealed in what another says and, instead, to listen carefully – sometimes even for the truth evidenced in what is not being said, but being communicated in other ways. Others will naturally be drawn to you for counsel, but you must be sure that loving wisdom is the source through which your counsel is gleaned.

Part of the shamanic life path involves mastery over the extremes of existence. Energetic highs followed by crushing fatigue, feeling taxed beyond your limits of body and mind, perhaps even an experience of near-death or symbolic death of the personality, a profoundly challenging illness in body or mind, or a period of spiritual darkness which eventually leads you to a healing rebirth, these are all possible ways that the shamanic soul can progress through its training. Such challenges are a form of initiation, teaching the soul to become able to consciously contain and channel energy according to its will, rather than being tossed about by the forces of the world. It takes time, but eventually the soul learns to live from a place of inner balance and spiritual grounding. The shaman is empowered to guide others through what has been mastered, moderating and containing what is required for healing. This evokes balance in the lives of those they touch.

Soul training in the shamanic way happens through your

life experiences. It may or may not involve official training as a shaman, but in some way you will be taught and guided by an initiated teacher. Training includes the experience of altered states of consciousness to feed the need of your soul to expand beyond the restrictions of everyday reality and feel genuinely connected and supported by a vaster spiritual reality. Altered states can include intuition, visions, hearing messages from Great Spirit, and an ability to recognise and interpret signs of higher guidance. This is preparation for dealing with forces that are not visible to most – and yet have palpable effect in the minds and hearts of many souls disconnected from their divine support system. Your altered states are fulfilling their intended purpose when they bring healing. When it is the right time for you, Great Spirit will bring you the necessary guides and teachers in the spiritual and the physical worlds, so that you can learn how to safely enter into and ground out of expanded states of awareness. This will increase your ability to hear and channel the messages of Great Spirit. Trust that your heart will recognise your true teachers – which will not always be those that claim to be your true teachers – as you participate fully in your unfolding journey with trust.

HEALING PROCESS
Find a place to sit where you can rest in silence or in the healing sounds of nature. If you prefer, rest with beautiful music (perhaps creating your own, with singing bowls or your voice). Allow the sounds that fill your ears – even if those sounds are silence – to be recognised as sacred.

Gently rub your ears, massaging lightly around the base of your ears, where they connect with your head. Then visualise, feel or pretend that your ears can relax ... the inside of the ears becoming relaxed ... the outside of your ears becoming relaxed.

Say aloud: *I release from my ears on all levels – physical, electrical and spiritual – anything that is not of the Divine. I release all lies and criticisms. I release all pain. I soften and let go so that my ears can become empty and ready to receive the healing comfort of great beloved Spirit. I invite in the truth of unconditional love, divine guidance and sacred silence now.*

Then rest. Imagine, feel or pretend that your ears can become so relaxed that they become pleasantly empty, empty of pressure, heat and tension. You may like to move your jaw around and open your mouth to help relax the ears. Then soften your face and, when you feel suitably relaxed, imagine, feel or pretend that a soft silence, which is the loving presence of Great Spirit, is with you completely now.

Stay here for as long as you wish.

You have completed your healing process.

22. INGONYAMA

Honour of the Ancient King

22. INGONYAMA
Honour of the Ancient King

The ancient king of the Zulu brings you an empowering message. You are destined to know and experience what it is to be truly empowered. Your voice, your courage, your wisdom and your dignity can create considerable spiritual light, uplifting and inspiring others, guiding them from a place of spiritual truth, towards the fulfilment of their own divine potential. If you have been doubting yourself, or feeling unworthy of the boldness of your visions, you must allow your spirit to roar, for you shall conquer all obstacles and succeed in your heart's desires.

IN A READING

This oracle indicates awakening and the healing and strengthening of divine masculine energy within the soul to take the initiative and to lead with wisdom. Healing of masculinity is relevant at both physical and psychological levels. To love and make peace with the masculine allows it to become dynamic and expressive of integrity, purpose, justice and protection. Acknowledge your own power – do not play small. Conserve your energy, get plenty of rest, but when the time is right, let your soul roar and your true voice be heard without hesitation or fear. You are a protector and leader of others. Allow your spiritual connection to awaken your courage and boldness. Refuse to be put down. Trust in the dignity and divinity within.

SPIRITUAL GUIDANCE

Ingonyama, in Zulu, refers to 'lion', yet it is not a simple translation. It also refers to a natural position of power. Implied in this is a position of kingly leadership, which entails the wisdom of justice and mercy. This is the spirit of the Divine Masculine actively expressed in order to right the wrongs of the world. This divine masculine potency within men and women defends the Sacred Feminine by putting in the energy, action and commitment required to bring her values to life. Divine masculine consciousness is essential for us to conquer procrastination, hesitation, fear, doubt and inertia. It is the power of the sword of discernment, integrity, strength and honesty. It is the ability to protect and defend what is worthy. It is not about dominating the world, but about moving powerfully amongst it, from a position of inner spiritual connection to the wisdom of the Sacred Feminine that is always revealing the way.

The oracle of Ingonyama brings you Lion medicine. Lion is an archetypal energy of raw power, strength and fearlessness. Lions carry powerful energy for those that need to be seen and heard in positions of leadership. Be fearless, and as you trust in the spiritual power – which is certainly more than enough for any divine purpose that needs to be accomplished – express your true voice and affirm your intentions. The voice of the Spirit is louder than any other voice within you or around you, it is the most powerful, the most far-reaching in impact, like the roar of the lion. This spiritual voice speaking truth will be heard and take effect, casting off any darkness seeking to impede your purpose and the purposes of those that you love and protect.

There is a time and place when the feminine must come to

the fore, and, likewise, when the masculine is required. This is not necessarily about men and women, but more about the masculine traits within both men and women. This is a time when you are asked to utilise masculine traits for best success. The feminine will then be able to flourish. These masculine traits include discernment and decisive action, creating order and clearing away what is no longer effective and allowing for the new to emerge from the space created. It may seem that you are being held to a higher standard than others. This is because you have greater potential to evoke an effect. Higher standards of inner accountability form a spiritual safeguard, so that power – which is so easily corruptible – is expressed in a way that increases light by serving Great Spirit, rather than our own (even well-meaning) agendas.

Ingonyama also brings the message of wise cultivation of energy. Lions can rest for twenty hours a day. When they need to act, they do. They also take their share of the food available without apology. If you have been associating leadership with overwork and have sacrificed of your needs to fulfil the needs of others, do away with that. In your wellbeing, strength and dignity, so much more shall be accomplished. Those that you are here to love, guide and protect will feel faith in their path all the more so when their guide expresses and embodies divine love and wisdom with kindness towards all, including compassion and respect for self.

HEALING PROCESS
Stand with your feet hip width apart, knees unlocked. Feel connected to your body as you imagine, feel or intend that your energy is now vital, golden and luminous. It shines out from your

heart and creates a potent field of divine light within you and around you, in all directions.

Within this light is the roar of the Divine Lion of Truth. Even if it seems silent, it can be felt, heard and takes divine effect far and wide. Allow the sound and the field of light to intermingle and extend as far as you wish, even reaching beyond time and space, into the past and the future, into worlds beyond the physical.

Say aloud: *Through the spiritual authority residing in my heart as the Christ Lion of Judea, I cast out the darkness of negative influence. I cast it out of myself, of my loved ones and my community. I cast it out of world events and future situations wherever this sanctified spiritual authority extends. May all leaders submit to wisdom, for the greatest good of all. Through the power of the Great Spirit of Love, it is done.*

Rest for as long as you need.

You have completed your healing process.

23. ABUELA MEDICINE

Remedy of the Grandmothers

23. ABUELA MEDICINE
Remedy of the Grandmothers

Believe in the formidable power of healing, of the transformation that it can provide for all aspects of your being and your life. Medicine comes in many forms from Great Spirit to facilitate healing of body, of mind and of soul. Whether it is the correction of unhelpful habits of thought, guidance for the practical steps to resolve a physical imbalance or deep soul healing that frees you into fulfilment of your divine potential, there is no limit to what can be healed through grace. A current of divine healing is flowing to you and through you now. Open yourself up to participate in a beautiful healing transformation.

IN A READING

You are on a healing journey. Put your trust in the divine genius of Great Spirit and the medicine of the earth, through which divine healing can express itself. As you allow your spiritual connection to guide your earthly steps, with synchronicity and divine intervention, you will be supported for a healing journey that will be profound for you. This oracle indicates a healing outcome that will enhance your soul journey. Your soul has healing gifts, and you are meant to participate fully in an exploration of healing that is of interest to you. You are meant to understand how it is that you are a healer in your own unique way (whether that be professionally or in how you are as a person in the world more generally), as part of your life journey.

SPIRITUAL GUIDANCE

Have you been the warrior, carrying on regardless of a deep wound that makes your life and work in the world more difficult? Whether the wound is of mind or body, there is guidance that it is time to allow for healing. Through a healing journey, you can become free to proceed more easily, effectively and joyfully in your life's work.

Grandmother medicine typically relates to the use of plants through various disciplines to promote healing of the mind and body. However, the oracle speaks of a broader interpretation. It indicates a time when earthly steps on your healing journey will be supported and guided by Spirit for truly inspiring results. Heaven and earth are intersecting, and when that happens, the practice of various types of physical-world medicine can become a channel for divine blessing. This divine integration of heaven and earth will transform the way you see and experience the physical world. It will provide you with a feeling of harmony between the celestial and the earthly, a sense of masculine and feminine energies working together for the same purpose. You will no longer feel divided within yourself, pulled in competing directions or conflicted about key aspects of your life and belief systems. This is healing – all things coming together in right order, working with rather than against each other, for loving higher purpose.

The commencement of the healing journey, whether you are the healer or the patient (or both), demands a period of purification, a cleansing that will support the release of toxins of body, mind and soul, so that true vitality, wellbeing and divine beauty can manifest unimpeded. The basis of all true healing is a shift in consciousness so powerful that it alters not only mind, but eventually soul and physiology, as well. If one attempts to shift consciousness without adequate preparation, the process can be destabilising, generating unnecessary disorder and confusion. Even if there is a temporary sense of heightened awareness at first, without adequate preparation, the experience will not be able to be integrated – and may result in feeling worse rather than better, without any real long-term change. Yet you are called at a soul level to enter a healing journey, so how can you avoid the pitfalls and open to the blessings?

Becoming ready for the medicine means preparing for the cure, also. This is based on approaching the power of earth with due respect. It is not about trying to force an outcome that you wish. It is about cleansing and opening the self to the gift of what is given from Earth Mother and Great Spirit. It is not about controlling the healing flow, but of readying oneself for it to be received. That means surrendering attachment and resting and cleansing the body and mind through practices that work for you, so that you are open to the certain change that healing will bring. It means practicing unconditional trust, because divine timing may sometimes express kindness through delays. It means gently but surely dislodging your belief in the fixed reality of your own experience, even if an issue has been present for decades, so that you are loose and limber, ready to be reformed, recreated through the healing genius of heaven and earth in intelligent creative relationship, expressing their unconditional love for you.

HEALING PROCESS

Connect with nature, in person if possible, or by looking at images such as the oracle card image, and listening to nature sounds if appropriate.

Imagine, feel or intend that you are relaxing not only your body and mind, but your soul too, relaxing and opening to the presence of the natural world. Allow yourself to feel held by this loving sacred energy, this is the soul of the Earth Mother.

When you are ready, say the following invocation, aloud if possible: *The divine healing presence is now created through the loving union of Earth Mother and Great Spirit. I surrender into the medicinal alchemy of divine love at work within all facets of my being now, so that any and all issues of my body, mind and soul that can benefit from divine healing are now blessed for recovery. Through grace of divine timing and compassion of Grandmother Healer, I ask to be shown clear steps for my healing benefit, that I may experience true healing and become a channel for such true healing in the world. So be it.*

Relax.

You have completed your healing process.

24. PUEO

Guardian of the Aumakua

No matter how compelling an experience of challenge, darkness or defeat may seem, you have divine protection and the promise of safe passage through to the dawn. You will see and hear truth of the light. You shall not be alone on this journey. Soul guides now help you find your true north. If you have been proceeding along a dangerous path, even unknowingly, Pueo will navigate you safely away from evil and ill-wishing, guiding you back to your higher purpose and sacred path.

IN A READING

Information that may have been hidden for a time will come to light. There is a guiding intelligence assisting you safely through a situation in your life that is otherwise confusing or dangerous for you. There are divine powers helping you in all situations to do with battles, unfairness or injustice, whether you are consciously aware of these things or not. Trust in the signs that you see and especially in the truth that you hear – sometimes beneath what is actually being said. The accuracy of your insights and perceptions are heightened at this time. *Aumakua*, in Hawaiian, refers to 'venerable ancestors'. This oracle also indicates that loved ones on the other side are sending you love and assistance, and are receiving your prayers and intentions for their own healing.

SPIRITUAL GUIDANCE

Through the form of Pueo, the guardian owl of Hawaii, invisible help from the spiritual worlds is with you, guiding and protecting you through spiritual warfare, seen and unseen. The concept of being in battle may seem far removed from what is, for many modern people, a fairly comfortable daily existence. Yet when we feel blocked from fulfilling our life purpose – whether due to a busy schedule, inner doubts, external obstacles or some other unknown reason – spiritual warfare is exactly what is taking place. Pueo comes to you with powerful protection for your soul during spiritual battle. Even when you cannot sense the spiritual light, it is with you, taking the form of allies in the realm of nature, soul and spirit to secure your safe passage through challenge and into fulfilment.

The Hawaiian legend of Pueo tells the story of a man, Oahu, who robbed an owl's nest. Upon hearing the sadness of the owl's protest, he was overcome by compassion and returned the precious items to the nest, revering the owl as a sacred creature worthy of respect and protection, honouring her as a divine being. This was considered blasphemous by the ruling law men, and Oahu's execution was ordered. As the execution was about to take place, owls began to gather, darkening the skies with their wings, making it impossible for the executioner to see or act – and Oahu walked free, protected by the sacred feminine that he had chosen to protect.

As spiritual beings we have great power to take from this world, to use and exploit the feminine world of soul and nature to suit our own personal agendas. Yet when we honour the soul realm as sacred, protect the feminine and recognise her divinity, we can trust in her generosity and assistance in return. When we forgo disrespect and theft, she will answer us with extraordinary reward. Pueo comes as a reminder that the soul realm of the divine feminine is real, powerfully active and influential in the earthly realm. Though impediments and restraints that have been imposed on you by the physical world may seem intimidating, and your mind may become enraged and want to dominate circumstances in response, Pueo brings reassurance. She is capable of overcoming the odds against you, freeing you to live the life you are spiritually destined to live. Have faith in that which you know to be sacred, even when those around you cannot recognise its true nature.

When the Divine Mother comes to you as Pueo, she also brings a warning to pay attention to anything that would undermine your joy, your sense of effectiveness in your purpose and anything or anyone that provides distraction or drains your vitality. Claim your right to life, and win the spiritual battle by honouring the necessity of your own soul expression. Allow her to use her lethal talons and unparalleled skills in the hunt to locate and destroy any influence that would lead to your demise. Be willing to trust, let go and change course – or affirm your current path and let nothing derail your progress – according to your inner soul guidance at this time.

HEALING PROCESS
You will need either a darkened room and/or a light eye cover (such as a small scarf) for this exercise. Find a place where you can feel safe and secure to rest quietly.

Say aloud: *I call upon the unconditionally loving protection of the Divine Mother. She contains the divine light, so that even in darkness, I am completely and divinely protected. I forgive myself and others now for all actions, thoughts and beliefs that led to betrayal of the soul. This forgiveness cleanses my heart and mind. I am now free to honour and respect the sacred order of life and have trust in my rightful divine place within that great order.*

Now it is time to rest. Cover your eyes or darken the room as you sink into a feeling of being held, as you rest deep into the darkness. You may like to imagine, feel, visualise or pretend that the great owl guardian Pueo silently flies around you. You may hear her screech. She hunts down what would harm you. She scares away enemies. You are safe, loved and protected.

When you are ready you will slowly return to the day-to-day world, stretch and move to ground yourself again.

You have completed your healing process.

25. ALOHA KE AKUA

Blessings of the Supreme Being

25. ALOHA KE AKUA
Blessings of the Supreme Being

Aloha Ke Akua. The Divine is love. The Supreme Being from which all of life emanates manifests a blessing for you. The realm of the heart is love's temple. When you enter the heart, you gain access to the Great One and to the 'mana', the power, authority, grace and magnetism to manifest your divine destiny. Trust in what is meant for you. Surrender doubt and disconnection in favour of love and respect for the Great One, and you shall live your true destiny with joy in your heart. Love can and will conquer all.

IN A READING

A blessing is coming to you now. Things do not need to be complicated. When you are confusing yourself with too many variables, too much information or fear and doubt, focus on filling your heart with love, and let everything else go. The Great One will handle all matters in your life if you open your heart to divine guidance and let go with faith. This will not make you passive, rather it will allow you to feel inspired to take only the most helpful actions. This oracle indicates an answered prayer and that the Divine One has you covered in a situation of concern to you. You are healing and deepening your relationship with the Divine.

SPIRITUAL GUIDANCE

You have an empowered and open heart that is capable of receiving divine presence. This is a sacred gift that must be protected. Protect the temple of your heart from becoming clouded by fear or lack of forgiveness. The purity and strength of your heart flows from your loving relationship with the Supreme Being, whatever your image of that being may be. Allow yourself to trust unconditionally in your divine relationship, and your affairs will work out beautifully.

Sometimes, we sense a significant purpose for our lives, a task that could benefit the greatest good. Or there may simply be an issue that you know you need to confront in order to grow spiritually, but your mind is afraid to let go. In such moments of doubt or concern, or even in those (perhaps slightly rarer) moments where you may feel like a super-being, capable of anything at all, it is important to remember the truth about the role of the Supreme Being in our hearts and our lives. We need to do our part to fulfil our destinies, and the Great One needs us to trust and allow for divine love to be our nourishment, divine grace to be our empowerment. The truth is, we cannot fulfil our divine destinies without mana. This is the authority, grace and power that the Divine has instilled within us and which will continue to help us cultivate and express through the guidance that we feel in our hearts. For every purpose that has been given you, there is also the divine gift of the power to accomplish it. It is only through divine relationship that we can tap into these gifts and make the sacred purpose for our lives a reality in the world.

You are one of the souls with a purpose and a heart big enough to be concerned about the spiritual vitality of the many. True spiritual purpose like this cannot be condensed into a job. It is a way of being. When you recognise that the Great One is in all things, has power beyond what the intellect can understand and is generous and empowering of the purpose of all souls, then you will be ready to express and grow your mana, your holy power, in the world.

There is a purpose for which you were born. Time and events shall converge to bring you to all that you need for fulfilment of this purpose. You shall gain all the benefit and be protected from derailment, as you deepen your heart connection to the Supreme Being, who is love. Cast aside anger, fear, disappointment and judgement. If you feel hesitant to trust because of certain ideas or past experiences, talk to the Great One about those things and ask to be shown how to find the peace and understanding that helps you become open to intimacy with the Divine. If you have to break through some barriers of mind and heart to love the Divine more fully, ask for help in doing so boldly. Acknowledge the divinity of the hand that works through yours. Do not lay false claim to the wonders that will flow (as that would simply scare your mind and close your heart as it wonders how it could ever do it again!). Instead, revel in the feelings of the safety, strength and tenderness that fill your soul when you allow yourself to pay due reverence to the Great Beloved.

HEALING PROCESS

Place one hand on your heart and say this prayer aloud: *Aloha Ke Akua. I honour and love you, Supreme Being, Great Beloved. I choose to allow you full access to my mind, my heart, my soul. I feel you in my heart now. I recognise your purpose and your power within this heart made sacred through your presence, now. Help me learn how to relate to you, to love and receive you fully. Please help me accomplish all that you have intended for me. May all serve your great loving purpose with joy and peace. So be it.*

You may like to spend some time in meditation, further prayer or rest now.

When you are ready, simply open your eyes. You have completed your healing process.

26. AMAROO

The Beautiful Place

Your dreams of a more beautiful world are not a product of childish fantasy, nor idle imagination. They are true spiritual visions inspired by the universal heart that yearns for divine paradise to be manifested in all worlds. You have a life purpose to assist in the creation of divine harmony in the world, through sacred activism and the expression of your soul talents. Believe that the beautiful world you long for is not only possible, but part of your spiritual responsibility to create.

IN A READING

Don't be scared to face a problem head on. You don't need to be wilful about a solution, but, in facing the issues, you shall simplify the complexity and recognise the practical steps that will create healing change. Keep your mind and heart open as you ask for unconditionally loving guidance as to how you best evoke divine healing in any situation. There is an outcome available to you that is far more beautiful and divinely inspired than what you can currently envision. Ask for divine help, and trust unconditionally in the assistance that will lead you away from the limitations of your current thinking, into the perfection of what the Divine wishes for you and our world.

SPIRITUAL GUIDANCE

It has been said that peace is not merely the absence of war. Earth Warriors understand that we need to fight for peace in this world, using our strength, courage, creativity, intelligence and will to continually align with the peaceful presence within. Saboteurs will want you to believe that peace is passive, that it involves denial or detachment from the world, that it isn't relevant, practical or helpful or doesn't create change – and that to rest in peace is some sort of unhealthy spiritual indulgence. They will try to convince you of these lies in order to keep you from accessing this powerful weapon against hate. A human being with peace in their heart sees more clearly, is more willing, able and effective in acting on their spiritual guidance, bringing a genuine and potent healing effect into the world. Such humans are harder to manipulate, distract and disempower.

'Amaroo' is a term used by the First Peoples of Australia to express the concept of paradise. In Aboriginal culture, there are said to be songlines that follow sacred pathways. stretching across the land. Each songline conveys a particular story through its song, and the language and interpretation of story shared in each songline is unique. It takes contributions from all of the many and varied groups within Aboriginal culture for the assembling of the songlines into a coherent whole to be possible. The songlines could only be understood in their entirety by an individual if that person spoke all the languages and understood all the cultural nuances encoded in its length.

The wisdom of the songlines can be instructive for the Amaroo Dreamers that we are, the ones who are passionate about creating paradise for all on earth. No one person can accomplish this on their own. If we work together, educating, encouraging, inspiring and helping each other – not only on a personal level and spiritually, but with intelligent connection that allows for interdisciplinary and intercultural conversations – we can, as a whole, learn to follow the sacred pathways of the earth. We can work with her to manifest a human culture that enhances and expresses her divine wisdom and beauty. We each do our part, together. We need inspired individuals who will engage with each other for our better and more beautiful world to continue to be birthed.

When we honour what we, ourselves, have to offer and are willing to share it with others and also honour what others have to offer and are willing to receive it, we will find fellow Earth Warriors, with kindred spirits and helping hands, in unexpected places. We will be able to assist each other in eschewing cynicism and boredom and, instead, we will learn things from each other, becoming informed and empowered. We will not believe in the lie that we are somehow a victim of the systems in place. Instead, we can be inspired by our ability to evoke the healing change needed through our own inner transformation, sharing our talents and encouraging others to be generous with their gifts. We rally each other to the fulfilment of divine purpose. We embrace the healing innovations that are already happening, and lend the power of our talents and resources, our voices and our support, only to that which belongs in paradise. Earth Warriors, there are enough of us now. We do not need to wait any longer. We are already working in many fields, ready for this moment of empowered creation and divine opportunity. We are the wild divine visionaries who not only see, but do. Let us continue to rally and rise.

HEALING PROCESS

Relax as you shift your awareness within.

Feel, visualise or imagine that you can see Earth Mother beneath you, as if your spirit was hovering above her. You can see, feel or sense the beautiful energetic songlines that weave themselves along sacred pathways, curving around our Mother Earth. Each songline is unique and essential. Each songline lends itself like an instrument in an orchestra, to the collective wisdom song of the Sacred Feminine. No songline demands that another be silenced or become the same. All the differences are required for the full beauty of the wisdom song to emerge.

When you are ready, say the following: *Let there be peace on earth. Let human culture on earth be a culture of encouragement, optimism, innovation, engagement, wisdom, reflection, community and guardianship of the planet and each other, for the spiritual benefit of all beings. Let this be now, that our future is the most blessed and beautiful vision of paradise. By the hand of the loving Supreme Being and our own free will, so be it.*

Place your hands in prayer at your heart and bow your head.

You have completed your healing process.

27. PONO PONO
Immeasurable Power of the Heart Way

27. PONO PONO

Immeasurable Power of the Heart Way

The heart has the power to heal in a way that the mind cannot understand. Do not allow your mind to distract or frighten you. You are a beautiful child of the Universe and divine love lives within your heart. A willing heart is all that you need to transform any situation that is troubling you. Recognising this power does not evoke feelings of pressure or anxiety, but, rather, of peace and joy. Lightness of heart and relief of mind are here for you now.

IN A READING

The Divine within your heart has the power to transform a situation that is troubling you. Do not be intimidated or think it is too much for you or the Divine to handle. Do not allow yourself to intellectualise or analyse a situation to the point of feeling confused or paralysed. Healing through the heart on any and all issues that have plagued you or a loved one can and will happen. Let your heart feel the faith it needs to feel so that it can rest in joy. Divine healing wants to flow abundantly for you. Open up to receive it without hesitation or condition.

SPIRITUAL GUIDANCE

Pono, in the Hawaiian tradition, has deep and multiple meanings, one expression of which is the return to order. There is a perfection of peace, beauty and fulfilment that the Divine has planned for the lives of all beings. Through the use of human free will, we have at times moved away from what is in the divine plan, stumbled on the path and become ensnared in terrible suffering and frightening delusion. This can become contagious, infecting other souls with the poison of hate, anger and fear, and further separating our human collective from the beautiful grace that the Divine has intended for us. It then becomes difficult to use our free will with wisdom, and our spiritual disconnection can create far-reaching negative impact for others and the planet. One only needs see the pain in the world to understand this. Yet there is a simple spiritual discipline that we can practice to restore the world – and all hearts within it – to rights again.

The Divine dwells in your heart as a healing power and wisdom, which tenderly alleviates suffering, liberating the body, mind and soul. This is the Immeasurable Power of the Heart Way. In the Hawaiian tradition from which it emerges, it is known as Ho'o Pono Pono or 'to set things right'. The heart power thrives through this simple four-step practice that can be done by anyone, anywhere, for any person or situation that they would wish to transform. This may seem unexpectedly easy, and it is. So why isn't everyone just doing this and healing the world right now? This is because only those who have come far enough on their spiritual path to have placed the heart wisdom above the dictates of the mind will be able to accept the practice.

The practice itself is not something that you can approach through the mind. The mind will resist it because it asks for us to take unconditional responsibility for everything that we encounter, whether it be in our own lives or out in the world, even if those situations seem to have nothing whatsoever to do with us. The moment something comes into our awareness, we are responsible for it. The mind can rebel at this, and say that it is unfair or unduly burdensome or shaming to think in that way. That is because the mind confuses responsibility with guilt and giving with deficit. The heart, though, is joyful at the prospect of spiritual responsibility, because it understands that it offers the empowerment to make a difference and that healing one helps heal all. This oracle foretells of great healing for you, as you open your heart to Pono.

HEALING PROCESS
Choose a person or situation to which you can offer healing.

Gaze at the image of the card. Recognise the heart power depicted. Place a hand on your heart as you tap into the beauty of your heart, including the feelings of compassion, goodwill and wanting all beings to know that they are loved and do not deserve to suffer. When you feel that heart connection, you are ready to complete the four simple steps, without them having to make sense to your mind. Feel the truth of what is happening in your heart, as you complete the process.

Step One – I'm Sorry
Say aloud: *I am responsible for this situation. I feel so sorry for this.* Let your heart be in compassion as you might feel the emotion that is evoked by what you are saying.

Step Two – Please forgive me
Ask for forgiveness. You don't need to think whom you are asking it of, just say: *Please forgive me.* As you speak these words, feel

the remorse you connected with in Step One. As you ask to be forgiven, those of you sensitive to energy may feel or sense a release of energy taking place.

Step Three – Thank you
Say: *Thank you*. Again, it doesn't matter if you have a sense of whom or what you are thanking. Before you even say the words, you may already feel the gratitude that begins to pour through you. This will increase as you say the words.

Step Four – I love you
Again, this will evoke a response in the soul, this time an outpouring of love. You may feel this consciously, but even if you don't, trust that it is happening. Just go with the process and say: *I love you*. Let yourself feel love as you say the words.

Place your hands in prayer and relax for a moment.

You have completed your healing process.

28. Q'ENTE

28. Q'ENTE

Sweet Paradox of Empowering Grace

When the mind says no, but the heart leaps with joy, we are ripe for a transmission of empowering grace. The sweet paradox is that the more impossible the situation appears to be, the more we are supported through grace – and our divine success manifests, swift and complete. Let the faith of the heart overcome doubt. Allow your mind to be filled with wonder at the unlimited power of the Divine, and you shall bear witness to sacred manifestation.

IN A READING

When there is something within your heart that you know you are on this planet to accomplish, you shall be given equal grace, power, talent and ability to succeed in that mission. This is the divine promise and sacred plan for you. If a miracle is required for success, then one shall be given. Pray with courage and confidence for your rightful divine inheritance, and allow your bold heart and loving soul to believe in your beautiful, hope-filled destiny.

SPIRITUAL GUIDANCE

Q'ente, the Sky Jewel of the Andes, brings you Hummingbird, who bears the soul medicine of spiritual grace, the evolution to conquer any obstacle and the extraordinary power of the heart. The concept of spiritual grace can be challenging to the mind. We often don't realise just how much we have been conditioned to subconsciously demand that progress in our lives be difficult, even whilst at a conscious level we bemoan the struggle and wish that things could be easier. We want help, but we believe that we are unworthy or have to earn our success completely off the back of our own efforts. Whilst the Divine wants us to engage and participate in the fulfilment of our destiny, if we do not surrender our arrogance and learn how to surrender spiritually, we will never fulfil our potential.

There is a way to allow for spiritual grace so that any obstacle can be surmounted, even the invisible ones that seem to block your progress from some unknown source. It is not a question of needing to become more powerful, but rather of your relationship to the Divine needing to become more vitalised. Then grace can flow, creating success in the same situations that would have otherwise defeated you.

When Hummingbird brings you medicine, you have a high spiritual destiny, one that is going to triumph against apparently insurmountable odds stacked against you. Hummingbirds have the highest metabolic rate of any animal on earth, with their hearts capable of beating at over a thousand beats per minute. These remarkable little creatures have an exceptionally high need for oxygen, yet some of the species have evolved to thrive in the low-oxygen, high-altitude environment of the Andes Mountains, flying at over 15,000 feet above sea level, in truly rarefied air.

This has become possible because of a seemingly tiny genetic mutation in how oxygen is metabolised in the blood. This subtle inner evolution opened up the power of some hummingbirds to thrive, quite literally, in higher worlds. Hummingbird medicine empowers the soul for success in situations that would seem the most unlikely. This medicine brings a subtle adjustment within the blood or feminine life force and how it receives and processes the enlivening presence of Spirit. This in turn leads to extraordinary and heightened abilities. Trust in the incredible possibilities that are birthed through the union of the sacred masculine and sacred feminine energies within you.

HEALING PROCESS

Rest quietly and be aware of your heart, as you place your hand there lightly.

Say aloud: *I call upon the sacred testimony of all perfected ones who have laid down their blood for the very purpose for which I have been born. I bear witness to their sacred testimony of love in the spiritual realms, as they call out for the cleansing of my bloodline. No impediment can stand against my divine fulfilment.*

Allow your heart to feel relaxed and peaceful.

Without it having to make logical sense, allow yourself to speak from the heart now, by saying: *I ask for divine forgiveness for my own transgressions and for the transgressions within my ancestral line, from the beginning of time. I open my heart with genuine remorse for all violations against love that I and my ancestors have ever made.*

Relax as you connect with your heart, and then continue by saying: *Pure sacrificial blood of the Sacred Heart has already been shed for our souls. The spiritual blood of unconditional love, beating in the living Sacred Heart, washes through my own heart and bloodline now, back to the beginning of time.*

This will evoke an energetic release from your blood, which you may feel if you are attuned to subtle energies. Rest and allow this to happen without attachment or analysis. Even if you don't consciously sense something taking place, it will be happening.

When you are ready, complete the process with the following statement: *Through the intercession of the divine blood testimony from the purest Sacred Heart, all impediments have been answered. Grace flows, and divine love manifests. So be it.*

Finish with your hands in prayer.

If there is an emotional release that follows this process, in your dreams or in your daily life, take a moment to place one hand on your heart, reconnecting with a feeling of love and peace within. Know that this is a continuation of the healing release and that it will subside, leaving more space for grace and fulfilment to flow through you.

You have completed your healing process.

29. NANA BULUKU

She Rests to Create

Your energy is a precious resource, and there are ways of being that can enhance it, amplifying it and replenishing it. Give yourself sufficient rest, and you shall find the way forward more effortless. Explore the lifestyle that grows your inner resources, rather than requiring constant exertion and exhaustion to accomplish an endless list of external pursuits. You need this shift in being now because you are ready to accomplish more. For this to take place, there needs to be less effort and more wisdom. Trust and value what can be accomplished through rest.

IN A READING

You have more than enough energy to bring to life the sacred visions held within your heart. An increase of energy and peacefulness is indicated. You are guided to choose high energy people, places and purposes. This does not necessarily mean that which is highly stimulating – rather, it refers to that which regenerates you with peacefulness and joy. Give generously to yourself to be able to give generously to others. You have unusual ideas or ways of being that suit you, but may not suit others. Work with what works for you best, without trying to force yourself to conform. This brings wellbeing and creative success.

SPIRITUAL GUIDANCE

Nana Buluku is the African Grandmother Creatrix, the supreme feminine creative principle. She created the Universe, then rested. The intersection of rest and extraordinary creative power is repeated in numerous spiritual traditions from varied cultures around the world. It is also repeated in the lives of inspirational innovators in varied fields of discipline from the sciences to the arts. When you are boldly ambitious and creatively confident for the fulfilment of your life purpose and heart-inspired plans, it may seem that rest is the last thing you have time for, there is so much to be accomplished. Yet the conscious use of deep rest allows us to connect closely to the divine creative genius. Taking time for renewing stillness can allow us to work smarter, rather than just always working harder.

African spirituality is based on a holistic worldview where no issue in one's life is separate from the spiritual worlds. This recognition that the Divine is intimately involved and lovingly invested in every single aspect of your life is how you begin to generate restful consciousness. This type of consciousness is based on trust that the Divine knows what you are here to do and wants to help you do it. Therefore, you don't have to orchestrate the details of your life, nor figure out everything (or anything) on your own. You do not need to have signs to prove something is happening every single day. What you need is faith in the fundamental good will that the Divine has towards you and your life purpose, the reason for which you chose life in the first place.

From that place of restful consciousness you can make profound progress. You can release striving and pursuit in favour of activity that comes from a place of inner inspiration, born from rest. In the mystical traditions of many cultures, that period of rest is considered to be the time when we incubate in silence and spaciousness. Through the invisible workings of the most willing and loving Great Spirit, all quiet and openness is responded to with renewed energy, clearer direction, and helpful guidance. You will likely find yourself becoming more active, and certainly more productive, through this process of resting regularly as part of your lifestyle. Rather than constantly discharging energy without having time to adequately restore yourself, instead, you will be regenerating more swiftly and deeply on all levels of your being and continually amplifying your energetic output. Your actions will have further reach. You'll have more to share with your loved ones. This is sacred subversion of established disorder that would otherwise have you chasing your tail, running yourself ragged and wearing yourself out in the belief that, somehow, this would help you get to where you want to be, to make the contribution that you want to make. Instead, you will be healing and growing and creating from a place of trust within, creating the new world order in harmony with divine genius.

HEALING PROCESS
Find a place to rest, lying down flat on your back, with your legs and arms slightly apart, preferably with soft lighting so that you can close your eyes. The aim is to create a restful environment that will feel supportive of you slowing down your thought processes and settling out of your head, into your body.

Gaze at the card image, noticing the soft circles that surround the head of the goddess. Allow your vision to soften and even become a little blurry as you slowly and gently shift your gaze from circle to circle. Do not focus sharply on anything, but just lightly and easily shift your gaze from left to right and right to left, up and down and down and up, from circle to circle. Do this slowly, until it feels lightly hypnotic and relaxing.

You are going to imagine, visualise, feel or pretend that your thoughts can drift out of your head, moving around outside of your head, becoming like the soft round circles. The more the thoughts become soft, round and gently moving outside of your head, the more peaceful and restful the inside of your head feels. You can relax more deeply for healing and restoration.

When you are ready, lay the card beside you and close your eyes. Rest for as long as feels good.

When you are ready to awaken from your rest, ground yourself with some physical movement, as you bring yourself back into the now.

You have completed your healing process.

30. PANTHERA

The Precious and Rare

Our faith and optimism are not meant to make us complacent, but, rather, to encourage us to believe that our action in the world will have a positive and real effect. There are situations where your voice, your courage and your fearless determination are needed. You will make a difference. Cast helplessness or despair aside and find the fighter within. Fight for that which needs defending with all of your heart. Do not yield.

IN A READING

You have the strength to handle any challenge, even the ones that intimidate you. You may feel that you are alone in the fight sometimes, but there are forces of good in Spirit and upon the earth that are fighting with you, supporting you, believing in you, assisting you and championing your success. It may not always feel like it, but you are not in this alone. There is help at hand to uncover a hidden piece of information which will allow truth and justice to prevail.

SPIRITUAL GUIDANCE

Do not give up on yourself or the Divine. You are not over-reacting or making things seem more important than they are in truth. When, in the face of possible loss, something deep in our soul recoils in horror, it is a sign that something is not right. It is not a sign that we are too attached or not trusting enough in the

Divine to figure everything out. It is a sign that we must fight to safeguard what would otherwise perish.

We are not here to be passive consumers of whatever the dominant mainstream consciousness tries to enact in the world. We are here to be the embodiment of loving consciousness – to be the fearless, determined enactors of wisdom. We are here to educate, to inform, to rebel and refuse, to speak up, to make waves and to honour the light in such a way that we protect and preserve what has real value in this world. The body, the earth and her creatures are not illusions. Saying that they are not real is not spiritual wisdom. That is an unholy deception perpetuated by the forces that don't want sacred activists derailing their devastating behaviours that place profit above all else.

Those of the Matsés tribe of South America are known as the Jaguar People. Exposure to outside influences and grabs for their land have changed their economy, introduced diseases and challenged the continuing existence of their culture. Their innate spiritual right to live as they choose has been violated. Short sightedness – such as in the exploitation of their lands for financial greed – is never part of the divine plan. We know this because the pure of heart recoil in horror and disgust at such events. We must not fall prey to the dark deception that tries to make us accept what is unacceptable by falsely attributing it to the Divine. The recoil of the heart lets us know that the Divine is not in that situation, and has not created that situation. It has been created through the operation of darkness in the misuse of human free will. The Divine is very much needed to correct and restore the situation before negative use of free will creates irreversible damage. We have the power to evoke that protective and corrective divine presence through the wise use of our own free will – which involves taking conscious action, whilst praying for courage, inspiration, assistance and protection. Such sacred activism builds self-esteem and boosts our belief in what is possible for wise and courageous people to create together. We become unwilling to be hoodwinked or be made to feel impotent in the face of unjust destruction. Instead, we rally and we rise. We gain energy, and we become fierce with divine healing energy.

Treasuring what is sacred, original and worth preserving in human culture is part of our task as those who are aware enough to recognise it. One of the tribal wisdoms of the Matsés people is that the best way to contribute is to do what one does best. There will be many who want to stop you, and yet Black Jaguar, a rare variant of the panther species of South America, brings the medicine of fearlessness and a willingness to act, the ability to discover hidden knowledge and unravel secrets. The Matsés and the black jaguar are rare and endangered, unique treasures upon this earth. Their presence in our consciousness reflects a conversation taking place between our soul and the Divine Mother. She knows how to heal any ills within her realm. All we need do is follow the urgings of our heart with confidence, and all that we need to know will be imparted, so that her beautiful will can be brought to bear.

HEALING PROCESS
Visualise, imagine or feel that there is a black jaguar emerging from the night sky. Moonlight shines on black fur. Fearless eyes shine like sunlit amber. The movement is measured, steady and without hesitation. You sense the absolute certainty and confidence emanating from this sacred creature.

Whatever it is that has been holding you back – whether you can clearly articulate it or not – is severed from your field by one deft swipe from Black Jaguar. Feel the release with peace in your heart.

Say aloud: *Spirit of Black Jaguar reveals my courage, conviction, purpose and passion. I am freed from constraint. I am made ready in this moment and for all moments to come, by the grace of the Divine Feminine. I am willing to participate fully in my life, to take action upon the divine urgings of my heart, for the greatest good. I will not be shamed and silenced. I will take action every day, in whatever ways I can, with fierce compassion in my heart and sacred rebellious fire in my belly. May divine purpose manifest through our willingness and talent and through our faith in ourselves, each other and the Divine. So be it.*

You have completed your healing process.

31. ELHAZ

Divine Might Foretold

31. ELHAZ
Divine Might Foretold

You know what is correct. You understand that any gain which comes from denying your values and compromising yourself creates a loss of soul. There are times when it may seem as though people who act without integrity are obtaining benefit without negative repercussions. Life can seem unfair if you limit yourself to a strictly human perspective. Yet nothing escapes the attention of the spiritual worlds. Restorative action and balancing fairness is always in action at a higher level, according to divine timing and wisdom. Stay true to your integrity, put your faith in divine justice, and you will win in a way that brings benefit to many.

IN A READING

Don't let yourself down with behaviour or attitudes that are unworthy of you. You have divinity within you and a right to be in the world with dignity, grace and integrity. Whether in a small matter of apparent insignificance to anyone other than yourself, or in big matters where you feel your soul, and perhaps the souls of others, are on the line, integrity will be your saving grace. You can be kind of heart, but also firm as you refuse to allow anyone or anything to convince you that lowering your standards of acceptable behaviour is warranted. Be in right relationship with yourself and the Divine. Justice will be always be done, whether you see it happening or not. Put your faith in the good and true, and you will successfully continue on your path. Others are relying on you to be true to yourself, more than you may realise. You are strong enough to live with honour.

SPIRITUAL GUIDANCE

The Norse runic teachings of Elhaz brings Elk wisdom. This is the soul quality of integrity which places you on the 'right' side of the spiritual laws of the Universe. In the Norse tradition, the qualities of personal luck, grace, power and the energy and ability to succeed are known as *hamingja*. This oracle foretells an increase in your hamingja, and in your capacity to impart your spiritual energy into your communities. This puts you in a position of increasing power and influence, which your integrity will help you express wisely.

In a position of spiritual influence, you will sometimes end up standing apart from others who may demonstrate less inner strength. By refusing to compromise what you know is true, you will be able to uplift those who are ready beyond ego limitations of greed, laziness and boredom. You can bring about a new understanding that one's standard of living is about more than personal ownership of possessions. Rather, it is about the inner state of our being and how we choose to live the life we have been given. Your influence is not about encouraging others to make the same choices that you have made for yourself, but about learning to honour their own integrity to make their own wise decisions. In this way, you become a spiritual protector and guardian of those in your communities, helping each individual to grow according to their own soul journey.

Elk urges us to care for and protect each other. We are urged to be firm about what is just and what is not correct – and yet also to be merciful and have compassion in our heart, for we are human beings who will stumble. If we are courageous enough to pursue a path of justice and truth, the Divine Father – an aspect which Elk wisdom expresses through the qualities of justice, nobility and integrity – will support and encourage us. The moment we are moved to harshness, even if we believe it is in pursuit of a noble cause, we lose our spiritual footing, compromise our values of mercy and compassion, and undermine our strength of leadership. In this advanced spiritual citizenship, we recognise that our empowerment comes from our consciousness. We use our will to uphold that consciousness, not to attempt to dominate another, but to evoke a quality of soul that inspires others towards taking their own healing actions.

Elk wisdom will, at some stage, bring us into a testing period during which we will feel challenged. We may question – or be questioned – as to whether we are being realistic or if we should just adopt the same lower-frequency approach as most others seem to do. In your heart, however, you know that the moment you do this, you would lose yourself. As we pass through this initiation of Elk wisdom, we will get to a place where, without any loss of passion for the healing outcome we desire, we realise that if we are willing to sell our soul to obtain results, then we have lost, not won. At this level of internal spiritual integrity, the Divine can rely upon you to be a faithful helper in this world for loving higher purpose. You are trustworthy, a true devotee to wisdom. And so the appearance of Elhaz foretells a successful and visible soul mission for you this lifetime.

HEALING PROCESS

Say the following aloud: *I honour the supreme Divine Father with love in my heart. I want to please you because I know that your purpose is fulfilment for all beings. I dedicate my heart to your heart, my will to your purpose and my soul to your spiritual care and protection. May I treasure the gift of integrity that enables me to feel for the truth of your presence through my choices and actions. I will listen to you, Father, hear you and not turn away. I receive your mercy and encouragement in the face of my stumbling, and so I forgive myself and others freely. I honour the power of your justice, discipline and truth, flowing as merciful correction through me and into the world. Thank you for trusting and loving me. I vow to honour and serve you with all of my heart and soul. So be it.*

Relax.

You have completed your healing process.

32. PACHA KARMAQ
32. Nourishment of the Soul

32. PACHA KARMAQ

Nourishment of the Soul

You are granted the gifts of fertility, creativity and earthly abundance to support all needs – for nourishing body, mind and soul and to live your life fully and be capable of manifesting your divine purpose. Give yourself permission to be nourished. This includes your body and also providing your heart, your mind, your soul with what they are hungry for – meaning, sweetness, divine love and permission to be authentic. When you feed yourself that which truly nourishes you, wisely and generously, you shall become one who can also feed the world that for which it truly hungers.

IN A READING

Explore and experiment with nutritional wisdom which suits your body at this time. Understand that it may change over time. Remember that caring for the needs of your body is more important and spiritually mature than trying to force your body to meet the expectations of a belief system outside of yourself. Don't starve yourself of what you need on any level of your being, including, peace, solitude, love, time spent in spiritual communion, artistic expression and nutrition. Answers are coming for your questions about all forms of nourishment, including nutrition, so do not give up when you are so close to finding your way. If you have been struggling with your needs being met on some level, a blessing is given to help you into more nourishing and abundant situations in all areas of your life.

SPIRITUAL GUIDANCE

So many human beings around the world suffer from undernourishment on physical, emotional and psychological levels. Being fed more of what you don't need cannot satisfy hunger. The cells and the soul cry out for what will truly stave off starvation. The quest for the profound vitalising and satisfying experience of genuine spiritual presence is part of this. Pacha Karmaq is known as the Father of the World in the Peruvian Ichma culture, which preceded the Inca tradition. He is the provider of the gift of agriculture. Part of his mythic story is that, in creating the first man and woman, he forgot to create food for them, also. When the man died, the woman cursed Pacha Karmaq, accusing him of neglect. In response, the god made her fertile. At a symbolic level this story tells of the need for sacred rage towards neglect and the creative resourcefulness that we can generate only when we get angry enough to demand healing change.

Food is a matter of spiritual importance. Without proper nourishment, which heals the body, illuminates and informs the mind, and fortifies the soul, we undermine a healthy relationship between the spirit, the mind and the body. If the body is out of balance and the mind filled with fear, then the attempts of the spirit to move your life in the correct direction will be met with resistance, anger and defiance. Denying the needs of the body out of a misplaced sense of spiritual consciousness is not going to further our spiritual cause on this planet.

Your sacred companions for your spirit this lifetime – your body, mind and soul – cannot fulfil their part of your divine destiny if they are not properly nurtured. This requires unlearning the social pressures to dominate the body and mind, and practicing guidance and responsiveness that has, at its heart, discipline balanced with loving relationship. Step by step, with moderation rather than fanaticism and by experimenting with what suits you – rather than what suits another – are ways to work with nourishment wisely. This may include changing our habits of food consumption to ethical, organic, local and sustainable produce as much as we can. It may be about willingness to redefine convenience to include that which contributes to health, rather than that which only saves time. It may also include noticing what we consume in the form of entertainment and information, and figuring out if it is really helping or hindering our spiritual growth. True spirituality is joyful and playful, it's not dour, and it's certainly not about no longer having any fun! What you will find as your spirit grows more present in your body and mind is that your sense of what used to be fun may not be so any more. You may need something that brings more joy into your heart and your world.

Finding what works for you can only happen as you begin to listen to the body, to your mind and your soul, listening as if your spirit were a caring and wise parent. Studies have shown that cows will naturally gravitate to the healthiest and most nutritionally rich grasses. Nature knows how to nourish and heal itself. Our bodies can guide us towards what they need for healing, as can our soul. As we recondition ourselves to listen rather than demand, we tap into the healing guidance of the Divine Feminine dwelling within us. What you derive pleasure from consuming at a physical, emotional and psychological level will shift as your relationship to yourself changes. Rather than it being an act of will to be healthy, as you move towards what brings you authentic fulfilment, it will begin to feel like an act of pleasure. Then you will be turning nourishment into a sacred act of honouring the gift of your body, mind and soul.

HEALING PROCESS

Say the following aloud: *From my spirit I say this truth: I am grateful for the gift of this mind, body and soul, which allow my spirit to experience the gift of a human life. May I be assisted in all ways to discover the best and most beautiful ways to nurture all aspects of myself. May that inner nurturing flow into all aspects of my life, helping to nurture all of life around me, through divine wisdom and grace. May all beings be fed with what is truly needed, through divine grace, and courageous, wise use of our free will as human beings. So be it.*

Place your hands in prayer at your heart.

You have finished your healing process.

33. INTIKHANA
Child of the Light

33. INTIKHANA
Child of the Light

There is a divine light that does not cast a shadow. Nor does it cast judgement, even though it reveals truth – a truth that is sometimes hard to acknowledge and requires that we change our ways. True divine light is healing, it is unifying, it brings hope and illumines the way. Other sorts of light exist on this planet that are not so pure, nor so helpful. Those sorts of light may appear stunningly bright, yet, in effect, create separation and increase ego. You can recognise genuine divine presence not by how dazzling it may appear at first, but by what your devotion to that divine light evokes in your heart and your world.

IN A READING

Trust your feeling over appearances. Move away from influences that create fear, negativity or doubt in you. Reach out for that which uplifts your heart. Spiritual protection is being offered. Refuse to be dazzled by ego masquerading as something spiritual. Through your prayers and efforts, spiritual light has been accumulating on the inner planes, even though you may not sense that consciously as yet. There will be an intersection of events and circumstances in your physical world through which that light shall pour forth and manifest itself as grace. Continue with your spiritual devotion. There is something truly good to come of it.

SPIRITUAL GUIDANCE

In the Incan tradition, Inti is the physical sun and the spiritual presence inherent in the sun's life-giving energy. Intikhana is the being who is one with Inti, a child of the sun. In the esoteric mystery schools, solar child and solar angel are terms for the soul, the deeper aspect of us that is connected to the spiritual light. This oracle brings you understanding that there is a new depth of soul connection opening up for you. We enter such a sacred process through a challenge known in spiritual traditions as initiation.

When we are faced with a deep unknowing – which is what happens when we are growing spiritually and moving through a spiritual initiation – we have outgrown what our minds are capable of providing. We need more knowledge, more wisdom, more light so that we can find our way through the darkness of initiation and into the blessing of new life waiting on the other side of the process. When we turn our attention to the soul, instead of applying logic and intellect to figure out yet another (doomed) plan to conquer the irrepressible evolution inherent in the spiritual path, we finally gain comfort. Hope is a quality of the soul. It allows us to bear the uncertainty when, according to a greater wisdom, there is something that we cannot know the answer to, at least for now. Hope gives us patience so that we can learn how to feel our soul connection more deeply, and grow into the wisdom of the answers we need. We stop fumbling about in the library of the intellect and, instead, seek out the answer from the source that can provide it, which is the illumined temple of our own soul.

Initiation often involves an element of the unexpected. We typically feel unprepared for it, even though at a soul level, we have been working towards it for a long time. If it's happening, however, then we are actually ready for it. Such spiritual testing is intimidating to the ego, but the soul knows how to move through the process. Trust your inner self, and trust in the light and the unconditionally supportive assistance that the Universe will lend to your purpose. Then you can be fearless, impervious to manipulation and remain steady and faithful in the face of challenge.

The solar festival of Inti was a celebration of new life, which was held at the start of a new planting season. It is realistic to cultivate hope and cheerfulness, both of which nurture the heart – especially during initiation. This oracle foretells of a positive conclusion of any initiation of soul. If you or a loved one have been plagued by dark and depressing thoughts, this oracle brings a spiritual intervention of joyful light. Open up to the joyful light of love and peace to fill your heart and your home. You have the power to call this in because you are acknowledged as a child of the light. Rest in the divine light within, imagining that you can peer into your soul and be warmed by the light and life of the inner sun that shines within your soul – which is the true light of Great Spirit. From that place of inner peace, luminous love and safe refuge, you can proceed with boldness, patience, wisdom and hope. The oracle asks you to cultivate a sense of self-worth and acknowledge the goodness within you, without needing to be perfect. You don't just have light within you. You are the light. Remember. Shine. We need you.

HEALING PROCESS

When you are ready, say the following invocation aloud: *I affirm the light within me. I call for the true light of the Divine to shine bright and clear, showing the way on Earth. I am the light, and the light is within me. I trust my soul and the spiritual light within that guides me always. May the light in all hearts be stirred into awakening with unconditional love, grace and mercy. So be it.*

You are encouraged to complete and ground this process with any light-affirming joyful movements – such as dancing, holding hands in prayer, opening your arms to the sky or simply meditating on the light within for as long as you wish. You may wish to sing or journal, say further prayers or create some art. Be with whatever affirms the truth of the light within for you in this moment.

You have completed your healing process.

34. ALAKOA

Spirit of the Warrior

34. ALAKOA
Spirit of the Warrior

Though you yearn for peace, you recognise that, without truth, genuine peace can never be. Even if it triggers an upheaval of transformation, the need to set things right is strong in you. This is the inner drive of the spiritual warrior, the compelling soul need to uphold truth, goodness and justice. You will fight for these things because that is your way, Spirit Warrior. Trust, see and feel the positive impact that you are making in the world. You are relentless and the Divine is within you.

IN A READING

Do not give up. If you feel hopelessness, despair, defeat or frustration, and you wonder if it is really worth it, place your mind in your heart and your heart in awareness of what it is that is inspiring you. Do you feel alone on your quest? Look for the legions of beings in spirit and upon the earth that fight alongside you, fearless and ferocious with love. Be uplifted by your fellow Spirit Warriors, beloved one. Feel the joy of their love and unity with you. You have access to the divine power that conquers any obstacle, wins every battle, and secures every victory.

SPIRITUAL GUIDANCE

From the fierce Hawaiian Koa tradition of warriors comes the word *alakoa*, which means 'to cultivate the spirit of the warrior'. Inherent in this code is service to a cause greater than the individual ego. For the Earth Warrior, that means a community, cause or country. For the Spirit Warrior, service is to higher consciousness itself. For the Spirit Warrior, love is the inspiration, the purpose for the battle and the only way to win the war. Joy is a sign that the Spirit Warrior is tuned into Source, for that is the frequency which lets us know when we are in divine presence. As soon as we are in the grip of darkness, joy disappears. Although the Spirit Warrior will experience emotions such as anger, grief and fear, there is recognition that the ability to conquer lies in the present moment and that fear comes from negative fantasies about the future. In disciplining the mind and nurturing the soul with spiritual light, the Spirit Warrior learns how to manage emotional content so that it becomes possible to be fully present.

The Spirit Warrior doesn't have a violent soul, but does have a powerful energy and a great need to put that energy to good use as an effective action-oriented presence for higher consciousness on earth. The Spirit Warrior within you needs to feel that your life is dedicated to something meaningful and magnificent, to witness the positive difference that you are creating through your actions.

Don't allow others to stop you from unleashing this beautiful divine masculine spirit power in your mind, your soul and our world. We need you! We need men and women who can surrender to the guiding wisdom of a higher power and get things done. The moment you deny yourself the right to be bold, present, practical and engaged with the world through your spiritual truth, your mind has begun repressing the warrior energy within you. Maybe it's your own mind that tells you that you shouldn't make waves, or that being spiritual means never causing a ruckus or that you should just be peaceful and let go, even though you know it is your heart and not your ego that is crying out for you to hold on. Maybe others are saying you feel too much or you should protect yourself and switch off from worrying about things that you can't change. Let your voracious warrior soul gobble up such lies and use them to intensify your passionate willingness to act.

If you try to repress the bold, dynamic vitality of the Spirit Warrior within, then it cannot function as it is meant to and becomes distorted. Signs of distorted warrior energy include the eruption into inexplicable aggression towards others with cold judgement and scathing criticism, or towards yourself in self-defeating, self-sabotaging, self-harming behaviours, in violent dreams and in feelings of having one's hands tied, needing to do something and yet feeling held back. If joy isn't cultivated, then the warrior energy can become dark and coercive, where despair leads to loss of integrity and the ends justify any means. True Spirit Warriors eschew such spiritual lawlessness. They have compassion for all people – especially those tainted by the forces of hate. They know that it is lower consciousness that they are fighting against, and that the people damaged by it are in need of spiritual truth and fierce compassion. If a Spirit Warrior tries to fight from a place of despair and darkness, doubt and hate, the battle will become destructive to their soul. When you fight for love from a place of joy, Spirit Warrior, the battle opens your beautiful fierce heart. It uplifts your mind and empowers your soul with the might of divine grace that accomplishes all pursuits and wins every war.

HEALING PROCESS

State your warrior's creed aloud: *The enemy shall never grip me. I shall not be overcome. I am led and protected by the greatest of all Spirit Warriors who leads love's army. My steps in the world are fierce with compassion and love in action. I waiver not, for I am a conqueror over darkness, spirit born, and empowered by the sacred. I embody the truth for which I fight. I am defended, uplifted and renewed. My hands are ever open to the replenishing power of grace. Great Spirit delivers all necessary might. Divine love's prophecy is read, spoken, enacted in all realms. If love has not yet won, then the battle is not yet over. And so I rise!*

You have completed your healing process.

35. MAMA QUILLA

Mandala of the Moon

35. MAMA QUILLA
Mandala of the Moon

I, the Lunar Mother, bring you my Mandala of the Moon to manifest through the law of magnetic attraction. My mandala is the sacred portal through which your dreams, intentions and visions shall pass into the wholeness of being, from the realm of inspiration into the world of form on earth. There is no need for doubt or concern, for even the appearance of delay signifies that the divine feminine mystery is at work, with timing unfolding according to a higher, loving wisdom. Trust that what is falling away is meant to be, whilst you have faith in new divine works being born.

IN A READING

This oracle brings a sign that creative works will reach fulfilment. Relax with trust and positive expectations that all your needs will be met. This makes it easier for abundance to flow and all earthly and spiritual matters to fall into place according to a great and loving higher intelligence. Things are changing, even if you cannot see the physical evidence of this as yet. Trust that your actions are leading you into a better way of life. Rely on the Universe, and you shall see how all things come together according to a timing and higher order that suits you, in ways even better than you could have imagined by yourself.

SPIRITUAL GUIDANCE

When we are very focused on something that we want to have happen, we can become impatient and try to control the process. We may logically assume which steps should come next, and if that fails to fall into place as we expected it would, we make further incorrect assumptions – such as believing that, if our plan has not worked out according to our current expectations, then that somehow must mean that it won't work out at all. The Lunar Mother is telling your soul that she knows of your intent. She is saying that you are permitted by the Divine to create what it is that you want to bring to life upon the earth, but that there are cycles of creation that must be honoured. She reminds you to trust in the sacred feminine wisdom expressed in the idea that it is darkest before the dawn. This wisdom is symbolically enacted in the natural world, whereby an ending and the uncertainty that can accompany it (the night) must fall, before the new cycle of creation (the day) can begin.

On a practical level, this guidance asks us to keep the faith, acting when we can act, and resting when we can rest. It guides us to not lose heart, even during times where not much seems to be happening. New Age circles often espouse the wisdom of following the path of least resistance, based on the Tao philosophy of ancient China. This wise teaching is often misinterpreted to mean that if things get difficult, one is on the wrong path. That would be a most unhelpful creed to live by, as it would cause you to turn away whenever things become challenging, rather than staying true to your path, no matter what may come.

A more useful interpretation of that wisdom is to not resist the natural cycle of creation. This means accepting the symbolic night, during which we cannot act, we cannot see, we have to rest and be patient, having faith that the day will dawn at the right time. So we do not insist that things manifest immediately according to our personal opinion about how, why, when and where. Instead, we believe that the Universe honours our right to create, and is working with us intelligently to bring to life the yearnings of our hearts.

The Divine has a destiny intended for you. When you surrender, you are led into it. Your spiritual destiny has been crafted for you alone, by the Source that created you, who knows you with extraordinary and unconditionally loving intimacy and wishes for your complete fulfilment with a passion that is both tender and fierce. We do all that we can do, and yet we know that we don't have to attempt to direct the Divine and its mysterious workings of love. Let the Divine Mother evoke peace and reassurance for your mind and heart, as you realise that her divine promise is here for you now. All things come in time, and for all things, including your dreams, there is a season.

HEALING PROCESS

Say the following aloud: *I honour the creative magnetism and loving power of attraction within me that calls into my life all good things, for all good purpose. What is not meant for me, I release with trust, and what is intended for me, I embrace with joy. I have been given the free will to create whatever I choose, with the understanding that spiritual responsibility for all my creations rests with me. I ask the unconditionally loving and merciful Divine Mother to guide me from the heart, that all my creations bring her pleasure and fulfil my soul. With gratitude, so be it.*

You can now express any heartfelt desires to the Divine Mother. Speak to her as a loving guide, mother and friend, telling her of what it is that your soul yearns for and knowing that she hears you with love. What you are speaking is becoming a prayer, so don't be hesitant. Give yourself permission to be authentic and free with your expression.

Gaze softly at the mandala depicted in the centre of the oracle card image. Gently note the circular outer form and the ornate square configuration in the centre. Relax. You are gaining healing from the Divine Mother as you do this. Let your gaze dwell upon the moon in her cycles and the sacred feminine figure in serene and joyful acceptance. Rest.

You have completed your healing process.

36. MAYU

Soma from the Galactic Heart

36. MAYU
Soma from the Galactic Heart

The Divine Mother's milk of the galaxy is feeding your soul. Expansion of your horizons, your spiritual purpose and your sacred responsibilities is taking place. Divine potential within you is awakening at a higher turn of the creative spiral of consciousness. This oracle is prophecy of ascension and grace.

IN A READING

Your soul has been going through a deep spiritual feeding process and is growing rapidly. The evidence of this in the outer world will be a sense of expansion of opportunity, reach, connections and new levels of spiritual experiences. This oracle foretells the welcoming in of a new phase in life. Newborn energies and fertility, whether biological, creative or psychological, are being stimulated. The oracle indicates the discovery, development and expression of talents. An increasingly public profile, which moves you into the spotlight, can help you fulfil your divine life mission, provided that you keep your inner connection to Spirit as the highest priority. The oracle speaks of soul healing around matters of trust, spirit, mother and abundance.

SPIRITUAL GUIDANCE

Mayu, Star Goddess of the Milky Way, was seen clearly in the skies of the ancient Incas. In Western traditions, the Milky Way is recognised as a metaphor for nourishment and the milk of the heavens. When she appears as an oracle, it is an omen of happiness, satisfaction and fulfilment. If you develop your spiritual practice, you shall come to experience feeling drunk on divine bliss, like a baby in an ecstasy of complete fulfilment through the mother's milk.

When we connect with the Galactic Heart, it is a sign of spiritual advancement. We are growing in such a way that our being becomes ready, willing and able to take up more spiritual space in the atmosphere. You will express that spiritual growth in your life according to your talents. If you are a thinker, your ideas will become more inspired, expansive and original. If you are a healer, you will experience the flow of a new quality of divine consciousness through your work. If you are a leader, you will experience a feeling of being overshadowed by something truly great, kind and helpful, whilst at the same time feeling more fearless, bold and confident to speak your truth and guide those in your care. Whatever the truth of our soul, encounters with the Galactic Heart are granted in order to evoke, expand and empower it upon the earth.

Some interpretations of the Vedas from ancient India see the Milky Way as the heavenly Soma, the nectar of immortality and the drink of the Divine. Soma can feed the soul, but like any food, healthy or otherwise, too much at any given time is hard to digest and can create more harm than good. More divine light and energy is not always better – at least, not when we try to take it all in at once. We need to learn when enough is enough, to detach from the Divine Mother's breast, and rest in contentment and fulfilment of the present moment.

To allow ourselves to be spiritually fed – to know when to latch on and when to detach from the inflow of spiritual energy, to allow for the mind, body and soul to adjust to the increased levels of light and spiritual nutrition and to metabolise that for healing growth – we need to feel trust and surrender into the Divine Feminine. If we have had difficult issues around trust, support and nourishment as human beings, then clearing those issues through grace, so as to be able to receive the heavenly nectar without greed or fear, is important. Mayu offers healing of these matters with grace.

Digestion and integration allow us to utilise the blessing and become ready for further expansion when it is time to be fed again. We trust that her sacred food will be available when needed. We can learn to rest into all that the Galactic Mother will provide for our soul, growing us into the fullness of our spiritual radiance and maturity, one dose of her extraordinary blessed Soma at a time.

HEALING PROCESS
Say this prayer aloud, with one hand on the heart, if possible:
I invoke the unconditional love of the Galactic Heart, and give thanks for all that is good, true and nourishing of my being on all levels through unconditional love. I surrender, with forgiveness and blessing, any issue to do with mothering or being mothered, whether too much or too little. I release myself from false guilt, shame and judgement, now. I release the mother figures in my life with forgiveness in my heart, for I no longer wish to hold on to old pain. I acknowledge I am worthy and deserving of nourishment straight from the sacred milk of unconditional love from the Galactic Mother. May all mothers receive healing and guidance, blessing and

assistance from the Divine Mother of all souls. With trust, I open myself now to receive what is needed for the ecstatic fulfilment of my own being, through divine grace. With gratitude, so it is.

Now it is time to close your eyes and rest for as long as feels good. Whether you wish to meditate or sleep or just close and rest your eyes for a time, give yourself permission to do that now. You can begin that process by gazing at the image on the card for a moment, gently focusing on the light at the heart centre of the Galactic Goddess and imagining, feeling, visualising or pretending that you are stepping right into that heart light as you either zone out into sleep, rest your eyes or meditate, now.

When you are ready, ground yourself with some deep cleansing breaths in and out as you emerge from your rest. Move your body a little and ground yourself in the here and now.

You have completed your healing process.

37. DIAMOND TIGER OF THE BLACK MOON

Second Chances Bring Success

Your soul is on the diamond path of spiritual growth. You may feel pressured by life at times, but at a higher level, those challenges are helping you realise your true strength of character. You have the personal will, strength and physical power that you need for success, no matter what has happened in the past. You are developing the spirit, passion and vitality to fight like a tigress defending her cubs. Believe in yourself. There is great dignity and strength in your heart.

IN A READING

Do not judge anything or anyone, including yourself and what you believe is possible, based on the past. Reclaim and redirect your energy according to what matters most to you. You are stronger than you may realise. The return of strength after a challenge, second chances for success and a brilliant intuition or insight that ends a long-lasting cycle of repeated struggle are indicated. A prophecy is given for empowered leadership, spiritual attainment and success after previous failure, which leads to an irreversible and positive outcome.

SPIRITUAL GUIDANCE

The struggles of your past were needed in order to grow. Yet now, having fulfilled their spiritual usefulness, they are no longer required. If you continue to interpret your life experiences through the filter of old beliefs and past happenings, you will lose the truth of what is taking place at a deeper level. You are being reformed, renewed, reborn, into a stronger, clearer, truer version of yourself. The past was needed to get you here, but it is no longer to be seen as something that defines you.

In astrology, the black moon refers to the unusual event of a second new moon in a month. As a sacred symbol in the language of the soul, the black moon represents either an emerging insight which you have previously been able to glimpse, but not fully grasp, or a situation that almost happened as desired, but didn't quite make the full journey from wish to reality. The insight or opportunity will arise again in your psyche to either reveal or ground fully this time around. Diamond wisdom is fulfilment and is absolute. With another chance, your breakthrough will be irreversible, diamond-like in nature, unable to be changed back into the state from which it has evolved.

Tiger medicine indicates a vibrant physical strength, vitality, and health. If you have been lacking in this, you are guided to tune into your cycles of rest, whilst shifting your mindset immediately to stop reinforcing negative self-talk (or internalising the perhaps well-meaning but unhelpful concerns of others). Instead, begin to speak to yourself and others of your vitality, radiance and power. Use your mind as your ally – consciously, intentionally and with an understanding of its powerful effect on your body. This is not about the mind dominating and ignoring the wisdom of the body.

This is about recognising and applying mind power to nourish and infuse your being through positive psychology.

Tiger medicine comes to you at a time when your engagement in the world is becoming more pronounced. Your influence is increasing, even whilst you may feel that you are being called into your spiritual path deeper and perhaps even with more solitude for a time. The divine beauty, dignity, strength and presence of your spiritual light is shining through, not only in your own soul and life, but it is beginning to touch the souls and lives of others, too. Tiger medicine evokes a sensual hunger for life and experience. When you bring your spiritual light into all of your worldly adventures, you will become able to create uplifting outcomes of grace that would otherwise not be possible. Tiger reminds us to have courage in the face of any challenge, any threat or danger, and to align with the truth of the Divine as our deepest ally, our greatest advocate, and our wisest advisor. From that secure inner spiritual foundation, we can leap with ferocious compassion, conquering any adversary in order to do what needs to be done in the world.

HEALING PROCESS

Repeat this invocation aloud: *I call upon the Divine Mother's gift of Tiger medicine for my body, mind and soul, through unconditional love, divine mercy and ancient wisdom. I honour the empowerment of strength, vitality, courage and truth. I invite this energy to flow within my body, mind and soul, through divine grace, that I may be ready for the path ahead, freed from the past with compassion and blessed in this moment with the joy of simply being alive. Through divine love and my own free will, so be it.*

Now you get to play at being a tiger. You can do this in a childlike way, crawling around and swishing your imaginary tail, stretching and clenching your fingers as though they were claws extending out of your palms (which are, of course, large, fluffy padded tiger paws). You can sense the ears on your head filled with sensitive hairs, which flick and pick up sound with exquisite sensitivity. You can feel how the energy is not concentrated in your tiger body in the same way it is in your human body. Maybe it is less concentrated in your head or your heart, and instead moving seamlessly, like a charged electrical field all over your entire body. You may feel the energy in every pore, along every hair, sensing the atmosphere around you like a million tiny hair-fingers. You may then sense a feeling of presence and vitality, wellbeing and aliveness, in a state of restful, awakened readiness. You may wish to move or to simply rest in this state for as long as feels right for you.

When you are ready, slip back into your human state, refreshed by your Tiger soul medicine.

You have completed your healing process.

38. PACHAMAMA

She with the Andean Emerald Heart

38. PACHAMAMA
She with the Andean Emerald Heart

Pachamama, the goddess of the earth honoured by the indigenous peoples of the Andes, holds space for many different creatures to live within her field – including the crazy, beautiful, dangerous and divine humanity. She knows that life thrives through diversity. She is able to foster life with such genius and generosity because there is no fear preventing her from holding space for the new to emerge. Be open to the new and the different in yourself and your life. Trust, like the Earth Mother, as an act of devotion. She is watching over you as you evolve to manifest the fullness of your sacred and original life purpose.

IN A READING

Don't hold back from what is happening. Things need to change, so let them change. It may seem chaotic or overwhelming, now. However, when you realise that you don't need to figure it all out, you will relax, allowing the wisdom of what is happening at a deeper level to unfold. Trust that your inner resources are enough and will grow to meet your needs for soul expression in the world. You may sometimes feel like you are juggling too many projects with too few arms. The Divine Mother can help you if you trust her to keep an eye on things and guide the process for you. This oracle indicates that peace and harmony will eventually triumph over conflict and challenge, bringing about a new way of being.

SPIRITUAL GUIDANCE

How is it that the boundless diversity of nature interacts as an extraordinary and harmonious eco-system, rather than dropping into a melee of competing interests, destructive conflict or soul-deadening, copy-cat conformity? It is all a question of holding space for it. The more diverse the input into any field, the more potential there is for conflict, yes, but also for creative innovation. Through our differences we can bring out the best in each other. We could also allow differences to bring out the worst in each other. If we do so, allowing them to close us down out of fear, we would stifle the uniqueness of the soul. If we cannot hold space for increasing diversity, we risk extinguishing our creative passion for originality, and then the energy, excitement and evolution that uniqueness evokes will be lost. Those of us in positions of spiritual leadership and sacred guardianship desire a more vitalising outcome for our communities. That means we need to tend to the way that we hold space.

For such an invisible concept, holding space has an extraordinary power. To tap into that power, we need to understand that we cannot hold for another what we cannot hold for ourselves. It has been said in Buddhist wisdom teachings that, without compassion for the self, there cannot ever truly be compassion for another. Modern psychology teaches us that we cannot love another before learning how to love ourselves. This is empowering. It means that we can grow as capable, new-world leaders and guardians of communities through the work that we do within.

It is reassuring to remember that the more we are able to hold a space for ourselves, the more we become a presence in which others can also flourish. As you do your inner work, your presence can create sacred space that is constructive, potent and transformative. Like ripples in the pond of consciousness, which emanate outward from the centre, the space you hold within can create a freeing and uplifting consciousness. Palpable in its effect, this will have a potential reach far beyond what you may expect.

As we grow in our role of sacred guardianship on this planet, the space we hold for ourselves and the world becomes more potent and important. That space can become a way for diversity to be either a beautiful orchestra or a cacophony of chaos. The outcome depends on our ability to hold a sacred feminine presence that allows for differences to be integrated into oneness, whilst understanding that oneness has nothing to do with sameness. You have the ability to bring great life to the souls of this world through honouring your own soul journey. Don't underestimate the importance of your inner work, nor the healing effect it initiates in the world.

HEALING PROCESS
This ritual is a simple version of the ritual offering of Challaco, which is a sprinkling upon the earth of a gift, done with the intention to feed and nourish the land. Begin by placing your hand on your heart and feeling the connection of your feet with the earth beneath you. Feel the breath of your body, the fluid warmth of the blood through your veins, the movement of your fingers and toes and the fluttering of your eyelids. You are alive.

Say aloud: *Ina Maka, my Earth Mother. Gaia. Mother Nature. Earth Goddess and Buddha of Equanimity. She with the Andean Emerald Heart. I offer my gratitude and reverence in this ritual to love, honour and nourish you.*

Place your hands on your heart. Feel or visualise that you are generating love and gratitude to offer to Pachamama. Reflecting upon your most precious life experiences or your love for nature might help you to evoke love, gratitude and happiness in your heart.

When you are ready, you are going to gently remove your hands from your heart, carrying with you those feelings which create the spiritual offering, and lightly sprinkling them on to the earth. Those spiritual offerings can lightly slide from your palms, along your fingertips, into the earth. Softly move your hands and fingers with the intent to release your gift into the earth. If you wish, you can also croon to her as you do this. Use loving, soothing words or tones or a chant that resonates with your soul.

When you feel this process has completed, finish with your hands in prayer.

You have completed your healing process.

39. ANKA

Kin of the Red Hawk Tribe

39. ANKA
Kin of the Red Hawk Tribe

On the wings of Red-tailed Hawk, a divine message comes. Your spiritual maturity has evolved into genuine power and discernment. You have earned your stripes. Acknowledgement is granted. Trust yourself and your destiny. You are ready. Trust in your sense of timing, which is excellent and inspired. Allow the Divine to support you as you hover, until the moment comes for you to fearlessly plunge into your forthcoming adventure.

IN A READING

A divine message is here for you now, so be open to the signs from the Universe. You are more mature spiritually than you may realise. You have an ability to share wisdom and honesty with your tribe. If you are still searching for your tribe, trust yourself. You will recognise them instinctively when you meet them, even if on the outside they seem different to you. You are seeing things clearly, so trust your vision and have patience. Speak your truth, but do so with compassion, because your words have greater influence than you may realise. When the moment is right, take action. A way will be shown for you to manifest your spiritual light in this world in practical ways.

SPIRITUAL GUIDANCE

There are some on the spiritual path that claim to be more evolved than others. Of course, these are likely to be the ones learning an important lesson in humility. Then there are the souls that know they have come with a special purpose – to lead, guide and inspire others – yet they do not feel this makes them in any way superior to another. It is simply the way by which they can fulfil their divine destiny. These are the Red-tailed Hawk tribe, and you are one of their own.

The red tail feathers only emerge in maturation, signifying that this bird of prey is a soul symbol for spiritual maturity in service to the tribe. This is also reflected by the red colour associated with their feathers and the base chakra from the Vedic tradition of India. Red is the colour of ground, earth, belonging, family and tribe, our material reality and the collective consciousness that we can create for each other to either move us forward as a race or hold each other back. Anka, or Hawk, is the medicine of the messenger. This is the one who sees and feels the birth of the new world and who recognises that which is outmoded and belongs only to the past. It is a progressive, honest, action-oriented medicine. As a channel between higher wisdom and earthly concerns, Anka brings a way to get things done in harmony with the Universe.

Red-tailed hawks are many in number, yet each one has a unique plumage. They are both an army and a group of individuals. So it is with your kindred soul tribe. You will have common purpose on this planet, but the way each in the tribe goes about fulfilling and expressing it will be unique. Our job is to recognise and support each other, even whilst we come from different disciplines, different backgrounds and are approaching the same world problems with different perspectives. We may work from different places, along different routes, for the one true purpose of birthing higher consciousness on this planet – but when we realise that we belong to each other in our common purpose (though sometimes it may be hiding under quirky differences of character and expression), we feel a sense of belonging, connected through an invisible but palpable thread of soul.

To fully embrace the supportive power of your soul tribe, both in the spiritual realms and the earthly world, you will feel the healing required around family, friends, and various types of community – including religious and business communities – where you have held wounding. Insecurities around being marked as an outcast, abandonment and rejection can create unconscious defensiveness that keeps people away. Once, you may have needed those psychological walls to hold you up, until you healed your wounds and grew strong enough to thrive through tearing them down. Anka comes with the message that you have outgrown those old ways. To continue with them will keep support away from you unnecessarily. You will clearly be able to see anything unwanted that used to be held at bay by the walls. You will now be able to deal with it through your skills of honest speech and your ability to tear away cords of connection or influence that do not serve you.

HEALING PROCESS
Begin by relaxing. Focus on your breath as you imagine, intend, feel or pretend that your awareness moves away from the everyday world and follows your breath into a sacred space within you and

all around you. Focus on the breath for at least ten breaths in and out.

You are now going to imagine, visualise or intend that there is a magnificent red-tailed hawk sitting atop an ancient, sacred spiritual book. The hawk is gazing steadily at you. You see that this book has your name upon the cover. The hawk suddenly alights from the book and the motion causes the book to open at a particular page. You are going to see, feel, absorb or read that page now with your soul. You may or may not see, hear or feel images and words. It may simply be that you are willing to remain open and allow the wisdom to soak straight into your soul.

When you are ready, relax and slowly begin to focus on your breath, grounding yourself by moving first your hands and feet, and then your whole body, as you come back into the here and now.

You have completed your healing process.

40. HI'AKA

Sorceress of Light

No enemy shall defeat you, not by night, nor by day, not upon the earth, nor in the soul. You are divinely protected and empowered. You shall fulfil your destiny with joy in your heart and laughter in your belly. Play. Be in nature. Feel the freedom of happiness within you even in this moment. These are your sacred powers, and, with them, you shall take every step upon your journey successfully, and nothing shall thwart your divine destiny.

IN A READING

Ask for healing, mentoring or assistance to support you now. This support will help you feel stronger and more empowered so as to deal with any challenge and be reassured that your spirit can handle it. There is spiritual protection for you now, as you follow the guidance to explore conscious movement and creative self-expression. This can stir up old energy, releasing it from you and allowing vital presence to take hold within you. You are going through an initiation in which you will need to reassert your happiness and joy any time it slips into the darkness of doubt, fear or anxiety. Take time to dance, sing, drum and affirm your aliveness with joy and courage. Become spiritually bolder in the face of anything that attempts to diminish you. Have faith in the power of the Divine Being, the Supreme Power. You are watched over by love.

SPIRITUAL GUIDANCE

Hi'aka, a goddess of Hawaii, watches over the sacred dancers of the hula and the arts of chant, sorcery and medicine. Hers is the medicine of light, sound and the ability to penetrate the darkness of lower-level consciousness which could overwhelm our sense of spirit, joy, heart and inspiration with defeatism, despair, boredom and even terror. This type of onslaught from darkness comes at certain times to those seeking to embody and enact the light on earth. One of these times may be when we are feeling strong and making progress, and we feel tested to sustain that higher level of being and awareness even through challenge. Another of these times may be when we feel weaker, more vulnerable, perhaps fatigued from a challenging time and just not quite able to summon the quality of joy on our own. In all such moments upon the Spirit Warriors' path of light, Hi'aka assists.

Hi'aka is said to dwell in a grove of *lehua* trees, which are sacred to her as the place where she spent her time dancing with the forest spirits. Hi'aka's name translates as 'she who lifts darkness'. 'Hi' is from lifting of the hip, and 'aka' means shadow. As patroness of sacred dancers, she reminds us that with a simple movement of our hip, we can move into the dance and connect with joy. It is said that one of the first things that a shaman will ask of a person who is plagued by demons – or, in our modern parlance, unable to summon the energy for their truthful fulfilment and sacred purpose in the world – is, 'When was the last time you danced?' Dancing, whether literally moving your body to music, or symbolically in whatever makes your being light up, is a way to invoke aliveness so that we can tap into the joy that counteracts darkness. Consider what makes you feel like your soul is dancing.

Make time and space for it in your life, as a practice for sustaining and strengthening your spirit.

Part of Hi'aka's divine purpose is bearing the clouds, providing rain, thunder and lightning. Her wisdom reminds us that movement in itself can be healing. When energy becomes stagnant, we can struggle. This doesn't mean we abstain from rest, because true rest allows energy to circulate through our being. This is why we emerge from rest feeling renewed and refreshed. Movement to circulate energy means flowing in relationship with our bodies, minds and souls, trusting our inner rhythms.

Most modern lifestyles make it difficult to live an honest relationship with the mind and body. It can be tricky to find the time and place to authentically and spontaneously honour our natural needs for expression and flow, so we summon our wisdom and creativity to find a way. Hi'aka says that we must. We must be willing to move with the storm wisdom within us, or we shall be moved by the storm wisdom around us. We will be moved by those events which startle us from our routine when we are falling asleep, rather than resting and living. Give yourself permission to explore a more authentic relationship with yourself, and trust that, in the process, the changes that will happen (and sometimes those changes will include how we live and work, where we live and with whom we share our lives) will be healing.

HEALING PROCESS
Here is a prayer of protection and affirmation. You can say this for yourself or 'over' another on their behalf. In that case, speak the invocation as if it was them speaking the prayer. This is a way to offer spiritual service to them. However, if you offer this for

another, know that you cannot force it to be received by their soul and you must honour their free will to choose how they wish to live.

Say aloud: *May light dance within my soul, lifting my mind from oppression and freeing my heart from restraint. May I honour my true nature and live my life with increasing honesty. May I attract endless divine love and the protection to live this gift of my life in perfect fulfilment on all levels. I am dignity. I am wild grace. I am unrestrained being. I move in authentic truth, dancing sacred joy upon this earth.*

You will know when you have truly spoken this prayer from the heart because you'll feel lighter, brighter, happier and safe. You can repeat it as often as you wish. As you do, the words will build a field of sacred light and divine protection within your consciousness.

You have completed your healing process.

41. MEDICINE HORSE

Progress on the Path

41. MEDICINE HORSE
Progress on the Path

I am Medicine Horse, bringing you the message of freedom, journey and progress. Do not act as you as though you are a beast of burden. Claim your innate divine dignity. Allow yourself to feel and be graceful. Recognise and honour your needs for rest, openness, safety and respect. An ability to hear, know and feel spiritual truth, which will guide you in every aspect of your life journey, is opening up. Connect with your spirit. Live your truth.

IN A READING

There is a powerful and sacred bond between your soul and the animal kingdom. If you have a beloved animal who has left this world for the spirit world, here is a message that this beautiful being is protected by Great Spirit and is loved and peaceful now. That creature is completely forgiven and completely forgiving. You are also guided to honour the inner knowing that flows naturally from your instincts and intuition. As you respect your inner guiding wisdom, your life experience will improve. You will successfully navigate your way around negativity. Healing, spirit communication and loving repair of the sense of self after any type of abuse is indicated. There is spiritual support and assistance for a journey ahead that will take you far. Progress is being made.

SPIRITUAL GUIDANCE

Medicine Horse brings healing gifts for the mind, body and soul. Horse is a healer. This oracle indicates that a time of significant healing is at hand. Sometimes the most powerful healing at a soul level happens subtly. It may involve emotional catharsis and dramatic psychological 'aha!' moments, but it often happens almost invisibly, without us realising how much our inner work is reshaping us from within. Eventually, we experience the fruits of our inner journey. Our interpretation of past experiences changes, empowering us to leave behind old points of view, former identities and negative expectations for the future. We begin to feel the lightness and promise of our spirit. We discover and take delight in our own divine beauty. We have made progress and a new horizon opens up.

Horse medicine also brings a special type of healing through two particular equine traits – authentic connection and heightened sensitivity. Many types of emotional damage to human beings can be healed through the experience of these two principles of Horse wisdom. It is the task of a spiritually aware and skilful counsellor – be that a human or a horse! – to mirror back one's emotional experience with authenticity, presence, honesty and acceptance in a way that builds a sense of real connection to another living being. Horse medicine is the soul medicine of trust – trust in oneself, trust in relationship, trust in our bodies, intuitions, instincts and in life itself, to guide us and provide us with what we need.

Humans can recognise and develop healing compassion for their own wounded tendency towards hyper-vigilance and defensiveness through witnessing the exquisite sensitivity of the horse. Witnessing the equine survival mechanism of the herd can help us address the wound around trust. Seeing herd behaviour may allow, perhaps for the first time as an adult, a person to honour the need for genuine connection and healing community at a deep level and see how vital it is to the ability to survive and thrive. When Medicine Horse comes to you, there is a deepening in your aliveness, a release of automatic reactivity and defensiveness, and an ability to be increasingly alive, authentic and real. You will believe more and more that the Universe has your back and has blessed you with the resources that you need, not only to survive but also to thrive. You will also understand that you do not need to take this journey alone.

Horse doesn't want to be held back in any way, and its appearance is a sign of progress being made in our physical, worldly pursuits – and especially in the inner process of soul healing. Horse medicine is helpful for cultivating a loving and respectful relationship with the body, rather than trying to dominate it with mind. It can help us in undoing patterns of abuse and learning to trust in bodily instincts and wisdom. It is also especially helpful medicine for developing a constructive attitude towards fear. Horse helps us acknowledge all our emotions, including fear, and contain them so that we feel heard, without censorship, yet also safe and held. We can then channel the vital energy of our emotions into conscious choices that allow for progress, vitality and engagement with the world.

HEALING PROCESS

For your healing process, use this simple visualisation: Feel, imagine or visualise a wild herd of horses. Hear the stomping of their hooves hitting the earth. Sense their energy, freedom, aliveness, playfulness, even excitement as they urge each other on, running together. They are safe, but they are wild and free. They are skittish and on the lookout for any situations to avoid, yet they are completely vital in the present moment. You may hear them snort or neigh as they run past you. You may sense the air and dust whipped up as their manes and tails fly in the wind. Can you allow that aliveness and vital presence to pulsate through you?

When you are ready, finish your visualisation with this simple prayer: *Spirit of the horse, beautiful, wild and free, you liberate me. You show me the truth of my experiences and that I responded as was natural for me then. Now, my nature is ready to be alive in a new way. I am ready to celebrate my spiritual beauty, the freedom to be myself and to enjoy sacred connections that are mutually supportive and encouraging. I honour you, Medicine Horse, for the beautiful gift you bring to relieve my soul. You help me walk in the way of Spirit, with honesty, power and grace. May all horses, and all creatures, be happy and free.*

You have completed your healing process.

42. KANYINI

In Each Other We Find Ourselves

42. KANYINI
In Each Other We Find Ourselves

There is a spiritual purpose that only you can fulfil. As you move forward on your journey, you create space for others to move along behind you, and as the ones ahead of you move forward, so too does room open up for your expansion. Upon this earth we are all building the sacred temple, each fulfilling our tasks as we assist and support each other in our collective divine mission. How can you help with your heart most actively engaged? What can you offer which inspires and energises you so much that others are uplifted in your presence? How can you receive from others joyfully, bringing them pleasure? Engage in giving and receiving deeply and with devotion. Your wisdom and openness to life generates healing for our Earth.

IN A READING

Healing is indicated, especially of wounds about connection and trust, safety and tribe, belonging and permission to be a unique individual. At a physical level, more vitality is indicated, and ample energy for healing. At a spiritual level, a deepening awareness of unified consciousness is opening up within you which will bring you into deeper divine communion and increase your effectiveness as a healing presence and sacred activist in this world. You have a destiny to fulfil, and there will be much help from many different people to fulfil it. The Universe wants you to succeed. Do not hesitate to ask and receive assistance, for your fulfilment of your own mission helps others.

SPIRITUAL GUIDANCE

The First Peoples of Australia recognise sacred connectedness between the spiritual and the earthly, and the bond that exists between all beings. They refer to this as *kanyini*. In South Africa, the concept of *ubuntu* describes a universal bond connecting all of humanity. Ubuntu and kanyini honour the understanding that the individual grows and develops, flourishes and expresses purpose and meaning in connection with the greater guiding purpose of the collective. To honour kanyini, to honour ubuntu, means to honour ourselves and each other as we seek out and fulfil our purpose for the greatest good. Our purpose is what brings our being to life, what we feel we must naturally do. There is loving and healing genius in the divine design and in the fulfilment of our authentic spiritual destiny. So are all beings assisted in the fulfilment of their destiny, too.

There are times when the spiritual path requires separation from a collective and the consciousness it holds. We may feel an internal disconnection from society during such phases, as we sift through the societal conditioning, casting aside that which does not strike us as truth and seeking alternative views. As we distil our consciousness, we discover a new way to be. Then, when it is time, we naturally seek to live and share this internal truth with others. We reach out to our tribe – or discover new tribes – integrating into the social fold with our precious offering of rarefied awareness. We realise that conflict with societal values serves a purpose. It helps us clarify our own consciousness, so we growing stronger spiritually, psychologically and emotionally. Our offering to our communities can then become a numinous alchemical wisdom.

A person in alignment with kanyini becomes a conduit for the intelligence of life itself. Their personal journey has a transpersonal effect. They become sacred activists at a deep level of being. Through their presence, things happen. They become a natural catalyst for healing transformation. A human enriched with ubuntu is open to others, encouraging of the good in other human beings. They are self-assured, knowing that they have an inviolable place and purpose in life. They understand that they can only gain from assisting others. So the spiritual progress of another person, and the sacred empowerment that comes from it, is inspirational, rather than a source of jealousy or self-doubt. In the Tibetan Buddhist tradition, the principles of kanyini and ubuntu are found in the Bodhisattva Vow, where great souls plunge themselves into sacred service for the spiritual liberation of all sentient beings. These teachings help us evolve from competition to the realisation that the moment another is oppressed, denied or diminished, suffering is released into the collective. The more sensitive we are spiritually, the more we recognise this – and the more motivated we become to serve the evolution of humanity for the benefit of all beings.

Kanyini reminds us that we can't thrive as a human being in isolation. Our humanity happens in connection with each other, through our relationship to the earth and Great Spirit. Spirit wants this for each one of us. We are provided the grace to heal wounds and open our hearts so that we can discover our belonging to each other and to the Divine – and through this, an authentic and compelling sense of devotion to purpose that heals our world.

HEALING PROCESS

Find a place to sit or lie comfortably. Imagine, feel or visualise that every being on the earth is being blessed by divine love. Silently, with reverence and joy, see every being captured within a circle of golden light. It wraps itself lovingly around the earth. Plants, animals, human beings, trees, bugs, lost souls and isolated humans – all beings are included in the divine encircling embrace. A feeling of peace, unity and healing builds within this circular field.

Rest here for as long as feels good. When you are ready, gently arise from your meditation and say: *May all beings know peace, divine love and merciful protection. May each one of us know true belonging and fulfil our sacred purpose with open hearts and willing minds. So be it.*

Place your hands in prayer and bow your head.

You have finished your healing process.

43. VIRACOCHA

Honour the Light

43. VIRACOCHA
Honour the Light

You are a light bearer. Your soul purpose is to redress the presence of darkness on this planet through shining the light. You are meant to do this in the ways that feel most uplifting to you. What brings brightness to your spirit? Do those things. How can you create a loving legacy to remind others of the light? Exploring and expressing the light in ways that remind others to seek the light, too, is a way to fulfil your divine destiny. Your light is powerful. Use it.

IN A READING

People around you, perhaps even you, can sometimes get caught up in the troubles of the world and forget to focus on the light and their own creative power. Gently, but persistently, remind yourself and others to ask for divine help. This can be done according to each individual's belief system. Prayers will be answered. Focus on the light at specific moments during each day. Place sacred objects in your line of vision so you see them and remember the light, often. You are a light worker, light bearer, one who is divinely designed to receive and transmit light for the benefit of humankind and Mother Earth. You have more influence in situations to bring about divine conclusions than you may realise. Don't be afraid to use your light in all ways possible.

SPIRITUAL GUIDANCE

The great creator deity in the pre-Inca tradition from the Andes region is Viracocha, who is said to have risen from Lake Titicaca during the time of darkness to bring forth light. He made the sun, moon, and the stars. In his wisdom teachings, this reminds us of the importance of creating numerous ways to experience and remember the light and to reflect it back to ourselves in the world. Creating things in our minds and our world to reflect the divine light is vital. These could be simple altars, sacred spaces, beautiful sacred objects – or if could be the act of burning incense, playing beautiful music, doing a daily practice of meditation and oracle readings, praying, conscious dance or art. Choose whatever it is that helps you honour the light and reinforces it as an authentic presence within your being. Through regular practice a radiance will be ignited and its flames fanned within. Our soul becomes a lighthouse to help others find their way.

Amplifying the inner light is a way to tap into your creative consciousness. Then, what you generate in this world through your thoughts and actions is what you actually want to share, that which increases hope, goodwill, happiness and peace in this world. It is said that Virococha made humans by breathing into stones, but his first creation efforts were not pleasing to him, so he destroyed them with a flood and began anew for a better result. The symbolism of this speaks of allowing our creative ideas to evolve. We do not need to be scared to let things fall away, to wash clean and start afresh with our creative intentions. We can do this daily, through prayer and other ways to honour and strengthen the inner light of spirit.

For someone like you – with a strong mind and the ability to broadcast thoughts and feelings more clearly than many around you, with a position and purpose of spiritual influence at a soul level – it is essential that you bring your mind and way of being back to the light many times each day. If you get into a dark mood, it doesn't only affect you. It may well bring down many others. Even if you are alone, hiding from the world under a bundle of blankets, your darkness doesn't go unnoticed, unfelt. The more you grow spiritually, the more your own states of being will have an impact in this world. This doesn't mean that you need to fear your own darkness. Rather, when it arises within you, your job is to recognise it and work through it without delay. You minimise the amount of time and grip that you give it in your own soul, and you practice authentically bringing yourself back to the light. There is no magic in this. It is an ability born of practice.

The discipline to practice comes from a desire to be in the light. You can choose to be in the light for whatever reason. It could be simply that it feels good or that it connects you to Great Spirit and you like that feeling. It may be that being happier makes you more attractive and magnetic to what you want to experience, or you want to brighten up someone's day, and not darken their mood with your own. You may want to show gratitude to the Divine, not discontent ... and so forth. The point is, that you figure out your best motivations to be in the light, and you practice putting yourself there again and again.

HEALING PROCESS

Say this prayer aloud: *I ask for divine blessing that my creations may be expressions of true spiritual light, bringing assistance to this world. I give thanks for the gift of my creativity and of my ability to feel and know the light. May this light dwell fully alive within me, inspiring my creativity so that I am a source of loving radiance for those in need in this world. May joy always be at home in my heart. Through my own free will, so be it.*

Then contemplate something that you would like to create or a feeling that you would like to experience more of in this world. Take a few moments to imagine, visualise, feel or pretend that you can build a light in your heart that holds all the good feelings and happy visions around this situation that you wish to bring to life in the world. When you are ready, imagine it rising up from your heart and flying towards the light of the sun, where it ignites into divine flame and returns to plant itself in the earth as golden seeds. Feel good about these seeds, knowing that they are strong and healthy and blessed and will grow into maturity, bringing nourishment for the greater good.

You have completed your healing process.

44. WHITE BUFFALO WOMAN

Hopeful Heart, See Her Sign

44. WHITE BUFFALO WOMAN
Hopeful Heart, See Her Sign

Have hope, for you are pure of heart, and White Buffalo Woman appears as the divine sign of rebirth and harmony. She is the way-shower who lives as one with Great Spirit. She teaches the practices that will free and empower us all. She heralds the birth of the divine upon a new Earth. You are held in her heart, and you will recognise her beautiful grace of spirit in your own.

IN A READING

This oracle signifies hope and reunion after a challenging or dark time. There will be harmony and a coming together in sacred purpose after putting pain or conflict behind you. A birth of something pure and true shall happen under the auspices of Great Spirit. Forgive yourself and others and lay claim to the purity and goodwill that is your heart's true nature. Spiritual blessing is bestowed. Your actions are in accord with heaven. Complete release and renewal shall take place. The good and true will triumph in the end. Have faith, for your prayers are being answered.

SPIRITUAL GUIDANCE

In the Native American tradition, the Sioux Mother, White Buffalo Woman, is a symbol of rebirth and spiritual promise. The story of her coming tells of two young men who witnessed her divine radiance. One watched with appropriate awe, whilst the other simply desired White Buffalo Woman's body and stretched his hand out to touch her. His disrespect cost him his life, as lightning struck him down – just as the correct recognition afforded the other man spiritual blessing. White Buffalo Woman evokes the restoration of the sacred. She demands respectful relationship with each other (whether you like the person or agree with their various worldviews is irrelevant) and requires that we each assume our rightful place in the community (which means not discounting your talents, nor trying to take a place by force).

For those of us attempting to awaken higher values in closed hearts that are unwilling to shift from more self-serving ways, White Buffalo Woman brings a message of divine justice. This is not about revenge or a mean-spirited definition of karma and people getting what they deserve, for if one is disconnected enough from the heart to be self-serving, then one is already in a living hell. The divine justice that White Buffalo Woman heralds is the restorative and correcting power of Great Spirit that will always find a way. If Great Spirit needs to use an unlikely candidate to do that, then it will. The Divine is not limited to what we think is going to work. It is powerful in ways that are beyond human comprehension. It is able to enact divine law and elicit restoration even when we wonder if it's all falling apart before our eyes.

This doesn't mean that we give up our fight, but, rather, that we are renewed with optimism and enthusiasm to embrace our journey with the greatest ally working alongside us. We find comfort knowing that Great Spirit is with us, not doing for us, but neither turning away from us in our need. We feel a more peaceful trust in the ultimate success of our purpose, for, no matter how many twists and turns the path takes, behind and in front of every unexpected obstacle, Great Spirit is present. Behind every at-first-unwanted adversary, through which we develop an important skill or deepen our unconditional reliance and trust in the Divine, Great Spirit is there.

For those of us that love the light and labour with great passion and perseverance, we need legitimate signs of hope to help us keep the faith in our progress and trust in the value of our contribution, for the evidence of good works is not always seen straight away. That the spiritual worlds love us enough to send us saviours is a testament to just how closely we are held and known in the divine heart. These divine beings help us when we are struggling to make the transition into the next stage of our spiritual evolution, individually and collectively. Saviour beings are our spiritual midwives, the birthing mothers and protective fathers who are guiding the human collective into spiritual maturity. White Buffalo Woman brings you the saving grace to progress spiritually and to know in your heart and soul that you shall see the sacred restored to its rightful place and spiritual harmony between heaven and earth.

HEALING PROCESS

With one hand on your heart, say aloud: *Such is your love, Great Spirit, that our every human need is anticipated. And in times when we have lost our way, you send us a saviour, one who loves us with such passion and purity that they are moved to action on our behalf. May we open our hearts to such saving grace and truly embrace your ways, Great Spirit, bringing the harmony of heaven to earth. Through my own free will and divine grace, so be it.*

If there are names of people – including yourself – who need a blessing of hope, healing and renewal, you can call for special assistance now by saying: *I call for special assistance of divine dispensation through unconditional love, divine redemption and mercy for...* (list your chosen names of people, places, communities, groups or situations, causes or creatures that move your heart).

Then simply place your hands in prayer at your heart and bow your head. If you can, imagine a powerful shining white buffalo within your heart, radiant and kind and rare, a sign of true hope, renewal and divine miracles of healing. Allow yourself to feel touched by the radiance, the other-worldly grace and beauty of this creature in your heart. He will fade away softly, spreading his presence out as light to all those on your list. Or, if you did not state a list, then he will spread his light to the world as a whole.

Rest for a moment in the bliss of this blessing.

You have completed your healing process.

Afterword

*Have faith. Be willing to take your journey. There is an abundance
of beauty and blessing from Great Spirit for every sacred path,
including yours. May you know the presence of the Great Spirit
within, and have the courage and joyful willingness to live from that
place of truth, bringing light into our world.*

What's next for you? You may like to play, study and train with
Alana. For those that want to empower their soul purpose,
explore Alana Fairchild's Soul Guidance and Sacred Mentoring
online healer training program and her many other offerings for
sacred healing and loving awakening at **www.alanafairchild.com**

About the Author

ALANA FAIRCHILD

When something is natural for you, especially if it has been that way since childhood, you can assume for a long time that it is natural for everyone. It took me some years to realise that my sensitivity, healing ability and natural conscious connection to the higher planes of spiritual guidance was unusual.

It wasn't long after that realisation that I stepped away from a career as a lawyer (spiritual law was always more interesting to me anyway) and I began my vocation as a spiritual healer and teacher.

From the earliest memories I have, I was always in conscious connection with Spirit. It has always been as natural as breathing to me and is probably the gift that I am most grateful for this lifetime – though I have gratitude for plenty.

As a young woman in my teens, I began exploring meditation and psychic work, and it was simultaneously like discovering a whole new world and one that I was somehow more familiar with too. In those inner worlds, I found a source of love, intelligence, humour and guidance that was incredibly kind and helpful. It changed my life. I wanted other people to have the opportunity to benefit from that loving guidance too, if they so chose. In my early twenties I began my work as a spiritual teacher and over the past two decades that has unfolded in some most beautiful and unexpected ways!

Now I live, breathe, write, sing, dance and create in honour of that loving guidance, to help its voice be heard in the hearts of those that are in need. This is the voice of the soul. It is the inner voice that honours you and all that you are, sees and encourages you to live with boldness and courage to become all that you can become.

You'll hear this voice in my books, DVDs, CDs and oracle decks. You'll hear it inside of your own heart, as though a tuning fork has been struck in the depths of your own being, and you'll realise that you don't need to be afraid. You just need to be alive and take your unique journey with trust. May you blossom and shine, dear one, into all that you can be, all that you are.

Visit Alana online at: **www.alanafairchild.com**

About the Artist

ISABEL BRYNA
"Mariposa Galactica"

I was born in California, USA and moved as a teenager to Latin America. Since then, I have lived most my life between Latin America and Hawaii. I'm inspired by cultural unity, our connection to the earth and the heavens and beyond, by the need for healing in the planet, and our awakening into a new paradigm where love is the living manifested vibration. I see the plants, animals, and all the natural elements of our world as my teachers.

Visit Isabel online at: **www.MariposaGalactica.etsy.com** or on Instagram: **@isabel_mariposa_galactica**

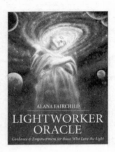

Lightworker Oracle

Alana Fairchild
Artwork by Mario Duguay

This deck is for those who feel an inner calling to connect with divine light and higher frequencies of consciousness to bring healing to the world. You can create a positive contribution to our planet, evolve spiritually, and develop your innate abilities to work with energy through different healing modalities, channelling, and communicating with higher beings such as angels, ascended masters and other spiritual guides. You can help humanity shift from fear to love.

You might already know you are a lightworker, or maybe you wonder if you are meant to be a healer or guide for others on their spiritual journey. If you are attracted to this deck, then your soul is telling you that you are a lightworker, and you have a life purpose that involves healing yourself and the Earth. *Lightworker Oracle* is designed to support your deeper awakening, empower you and encourage you to fulfil your divine life purpose.

ISBN: 978-1-925538-00-7
44 cards and 140-page guidebook set, packaged in a hardcover box.

ALSO AVAILABLE FROM BLUE ANGEL PUBLISHING®

Love Your Inner Goddess
(Gift Book & CD/MP3 kit)

Alana Fairchild
Artwork by Lisa Ferrante

Loving your inner goddess means giving back to you, as you learn how to nurture yourself. Explore sacred feminine play and healing as your inner goddess shines and shows you how to respect yourself, feel vital and enjoy your unique beauty.

Awaken and express your divine feminine spirit with these fun, quick and enjoyable techniques to nourish your soul and enhance your emotional wellbeing. Your loved-up inner goddess will inspire you to ...

· Express yourself authentically
· Be empowered and self-confident
· Ignite your creativity
· Trust your intuition
· Feel attractive and radiant (that's your inner goddess glow!)
· Shine with positive energy

Enjoy music, meditation, sacred rituals and spiritual guidance as you discover the powers of your inner goddess. Celebrate the exotic, empowered goddess within you!

ISBN: 978-1-925538-07-6
100-page book with CD and MP3 download card.

Rumi Oracle
An Invitation into the Heart of the Divine

Alana Fairchild
Artwork by Rassouli

Rumi speaks a sacred language that we understand with our hearts rather than our minds. He knows the heart is the gateway to divine union and he doesn't want you to play small this lifetime. He encourages humanity to live and love with absolute surrender, abandon and willingness to accept the mysteries of life.

Whether you have studied his poetry for years or are drawn to him only now, this oracle deck will strengthen and illuminate your connection with this beautiful and powerful soul who loves you with a fierce passion.

Rumi has a heart so open that the entire world that he loves so dearly can easily be held within it. His is a path of love. To dance in divine love with him, you need only be willing to enter your own heart. May the blessings of this spiritual brother lead you into the bliss of your own divine heart-centred nature.

ISBN: 978-1-922161-68-0
44 cards and 204-page guidebook set, packaged in a hardcover box.

Sacred Rebels Oracle
Guidance for Living a Unique & Authentic Life

Alana Fairchild
Artwork by Autumn Skye Morrison

This stunning deck is dedicated to YOU – you who want to live your own, unique, inspired life, and share your light with the world as a sacred offering.

Sacred Rebels Oracle is for those that are ready to celebrate and nurture their individuality. When you are a Sacred Rebel you want to be fully alive and express your authentic truths. You want to help heal the world, even when that means shaking things up. Sacred Rebels love life and refuse to believe that manifesting their dreams is impossible!

This oracle deck is filled with striking imagery and beautiful heartfelt guidance to support you in awakening your sacred rebellious heart, so that you will trust in your own uniqueness and authenticity, and honour your own creative power.

ISBN: 978-1-922161-33-8
45 cards and 184-page guidebook set, packaged in a hardcover box.

For more information on this
or any Blue Angel Publishing release,
please visit our website at:

www.blueangelonline.com